2006

WOMEN AROUND THE WORLD ARE REMODELING THEIR REALITIES!

"It's so easy to lose yourself amidst the responsibilities in your life—career, family, relationships. Working with Kim and *Remodel Your Reality*, I've rediscovered myself and my purpose. **This is the best money I've ever spent.**"

Susan
Healthcare Executive, Aunt, Sister

"Before working through this program, my business was monopolizing my time. I was not satisfied with my marriage, was dissatisfied with my weight, and simply wasn't happy. Working through the program, I have learned that I can take a leap of faith anywhere in my life and have things turn out the way I intend. I learned to ask for what I want in my marriage and have started to make time to care for my body. My business and relationships are better than they've ever been. I've finally accepted that I can have it all and that **I DESERVE it all!** Thank you, Kim, for making a huge contribution to my life!"

Sandra
Business Owner, Wife, Mother

"Before coaching, I lacked passion and excitement. As a result of working through this program, I have learned to tap into my courage and identify what I value and need in my life. I've also learned how to make sure I'm getting what I need from family and friends. By being true to my needs and values, I'm truly happy again, which makes the important people in my life happy too."

Leigh Ann
Business Development Manager, Wife, Mother

"When I started this program, I lacked focus and felt stuck. This work has had a powerful impact in my life. I have developed focus and defined goals for key areas of my life. Kim helped me design an action plan to support the achievement of these goals, and her understanding style made the difference between staying 'stuck' and having a paradigm shift! For anyone interested in moving her life forward, I highly recommend Kim Fulcher and *Remodel Your Reality!*"

Kathy
Business Owner, Environmental Activist

"Before I invested in this program, I lacked motivation and doubted my ability to achieve what I wanted. Through each step, I rediscovered my passion and the drive I once had to succeed in my career. My passion carried over into every aspect of my life: my husband, my family, my home, and my career. Now I know myself, so I can really live life!"

Cheryl
Financial Consultant, Wife, Mother

"When I started this program, I was frustrated with losing and regaining the same twenty pounds over and over again. While working with this program, I learned what was driving me to eat. I took steps to take care of myself emotionally, physically, and spiritually. Today, I am five pounds away from my goal weight, I like myself, and I love my life. Thank you, Kim and *Remodel Your Reality*, for the difference you've made in my life!"

Cameron
Sales Director, Wife, Mother

"I am so amazed at where I am since starting this program! When I look at the progress I've made in such a VERY short time, I realize how truly fortunate I am to have 'stumbled' across *Remodel Your Reality*. I will be forever thankful!"

Julie
Administrator, Wife, Mother

"When I began the *Remodel Your Reality* process, I was unhappy with my job and my relationship. After working through this program with Kim as my personal coach, I have found the job of my dreams, increased my salary by over $20K, and ended a relationship that wasn't meeting my needs. I am filled with energy and am working toward clear goals. This program changed my life!"

Cristina
Marketing Manager, Daughter, Aunt

"Before I started working through this program, I was a serial entrepreneur who always quit before I finished what I started. I had a serious fear of failure, and I was stuck. Since completing this program, I have realized that I am strong enough to walk through my fear. As a result of working through *Remodel Your Reality*, I have successfully started my own business. Fear is no longer an obstacle, but a stepping stone!"

Wendi
Small Business Owner, Wife, Mother

"I started the *Remodel Your Reality* process because I wanted to make changes in my career. As a result of working through this program I have recruited six new sales associates, developed a new training program, improved my ability to communicate, and am much more effective in every facet of my business. I strongly recommend this program to any woman looking to change her life! You can't afford not to buy this book!"

Giny
Regional Sales Leader, Grandmother, Mentor

"When I invested in *Remodel Your Reality* I lacked confidence in my ability to have the career of my dreams, and I needed help building my client base. Since completing this program I have learned valuable lessons that I know will serve me for the rest of my life. I am now fully aware of the obstacles that keep me stuck, and I know how to overcome them. I have doubled my income, strengthened my professional skills, and embraced all aspects of my life. Thank you, Kim, for the *Remodel Your Reality* process!"

Deb
Small Business Owner, Wife, Friend

"Before doing this work I was dissatisfied with my career. After doing the work, I have come to understand that I was not being challenged, and I understand why I was so unhappy. I have found the courage to go for the kind of career I dream of having, and I'm excited to say that I begin a new position next week! I'm looking forward to my new job. I feel excited again, and—most important—I'm ready to explore! Thanks again!"

Jennifer
Newly Single Engineer

ARE YOU READY TO RECLAIM YOUR LIFE AND FEEL EXCITED, PASSIONATE, AND ENERGIZED?

How often do you feel like you're actually in control of your day, much less in control of your life?

Do you think the "realities" of life make living your dreams impractical, if not downright impossible?

Think again.

It's possible you've lost track of the fact that what you call the *demands* of each day—at work, at home, in relationships, with family—are actually *choices* you make. *Remodel Your Reality* reveals practical ways you can begin to consistently make choices that support what you *want* so you stop feeling swept along by what you *think* you need to do.

Life coach Kimberly Fulcher has developed an experience-tested, 7-step approach to help you create balance in your life. It works—even amidst the chaos of today's fast-paced world. In clear, simple terms it shows you how to reclaim your energy and effectively maximize the abundant possibility within your life. It assists you in getting back in touch with and clarifying what you really want, and shows you how to make your dreams a reality—starting right where you are in life. Kim takes your hand and coaches you through the process she's used with her clients for years.

The promise of this program is nothing short of a transformation of your life. The simple steps will keep you nodding your head and turning pages. The fascinating case histories of women who have successfully applied its principles will encourage you, and as you find out how easy it is to integrate the program into your own life you will feel excitement, joy, and a budding passion. *Remodel Your Reality* will make you a happier, healthier, more fulfilled woman.

Prepare to fall in love with your life, reconnect with the wonderful woman you are, and awaken the powerful potential that lives within you.

Kimberly Fulcher lives the kind of life she writes about. She is a highly regarded entrepreneur, business leader, author, speaker, and life coach. As the founder of Compass, Inc., a coaching company, she works with clients ranging from corporate CEOs to homemakers. Kim has gained national recognition as an expert in personal and professional success. She is happily married and the proud parent of four children. Kim has created a balanced life in which she loves working with her clients and spending time between her home in California and her ranch in Washington State.

REMODEL YOUR REALITY

A Book For Women Whose Lives Have Taken Over Their Dreams

REMODEL
YOUR
REALITY

Seven Steps to

Rebalance

Your Life

and Reclaim

Your Passion

KIMBERLY FULCHER

River Rock Press

This publication is designed to educate and provide general information regarding the subject matter covered. It is not intended to replace the counsel of other professional advisors. The reader is encouraged to consult with his or her own advisors regarding specific situations. While the author has taken reasonable precautions in the preparation of this book and believes the facts presented within the book are accurate, neither the publisher nor author assumes any responsibility for errors or omissions. The author and publisher specifically disclaim any liability resulting from the use or application of the information contained in this book. The information within this book is not intended to serve as emotional or therapeutic advice related to individual situations.

River Rock Press
5655 Silver Creek Valley Road, Suite 403
San Jose, CA 95138
Toll free: 866-341-8618
Fax: 877-675-3126
www.mylifecompass.com
customerservice@mylifecompass.com

Printed in the United States of America on acid-free paper.

Publisher's Cataloging-In-Publication

Fulcher, Kimberly.
    Remodel your reality: seven steps to rebalance your life and reclaim your passion / Kimberly Fulcher. -- 1st ed. -- San Jose, CA : River Rock Press, 2006.
        p. ; cm.
    "A book for women whose lives have taken over their dreams."
    Includes index.
    ISBN: 978-09770260-4-3

    1. Quality of life. 2. Women--Identity. 3. Stress management for women. 4. Relaxation. 5. Women--Mental health. 6. Women--Health and hygiene. 7. Women--Psychology. I. Title.

HQ2037 .F85   2006 2005905676
155.6/33--dc22   0604

Book Design: Patricia Bacall
Cover Photo: Kathleen Reeve
Editing: Brookes Nohlgren
Indexing: Gina Gerboth
Book Consultant: Ellen Reid

To Jay—my husband, my best friend, my partner in life. Because of your love and acceptance, I've embraced all aspects of who I am. This book is a result of your constant support, endorsement, and encouragement. Thank you for believing in me, for loving me, and for challenging me to brush up against my potential. You are everything a man should be, and I love you.

Table of Contents

Introduction | Step into Balance   xxi

Part I   Manage Your Energy

Step 1 | Reclaim Your Energy: The Three Factors
of Vitality   3

Step 2 | Align Your Focus: The Priority Compass   35

Part II   Establish Your Foundation

Step 3 | Define What Drives You: The Power
of Needs and Beliefs   57

Step 4 | Light Your Fire: The Passion Triad   85

Part III   Develop Your Dream

Step 5 | Stake Your Claim: The Life
of Your Dreams Is Within Reach   107

Step 6 | Establish Key Connections:
Rich Relationships   129

Step 7 | Stay Your Course: The Tenets
of Personal Effectiveness   163

Keep Stepping | Living in Balance   179

Index   187

ACKNOWLEDGEMENTS

This book is the result of a long and fruitful journey. It would not have been possible without the team of loving, creative, and talented people who supported and guided me each step of the way.

In particular I'd like to thank Thomas Leonard, the founding father of the coaching profession, an industry that has provided a home for me and so many others like me, who are deeply committed to helping others live happy, productive, fulfilled lives. While his time on Earth has ended, his vision lives on. Thank you for giving this wonderful profession of ours a foundation to build on.

I'd like to thank Ellen Reid, the Book Shepherd, who so beautifully orchestrated the birth of this book. Thank you for your vision, your no-nonsense advice, and your incredibly talented team. Special thanks to Laren Bright, Brookes Nohlgren, Patricia Bacall, and Gina Gerboth for helping to turn this manuscript into a book that I hope will touch and inspire many lives.

To the Compass Team, thank you! Your enthusiasm, energy, and unflagging commitment to our work is incredibly gratifying. Marie, you are one of the most solid, dependable, and creative women I've ever met. Because of you, Compass operates like a well-oiled machine. Thank you! Helaine, Cheryl, and Shawn, thank you for your willingness to take a risk. Each day I make a commitment to deliver on the faith you have invested in Compass. Jackie and Tammy, thank you for being great partners. The work we've done together has been enlightening, and I know we've only just begun.

To my clients—thank you! You have allowed me to share in the most intimate parts of your lives. Your trust, courage, perseverance, and willingness to reach for the life of your dreams has astounded me. I have learned from each of you and commit each day to building upon your wisdom and strength. I so appreciate your willingness to include me in your journey!

Finally, I want to thank my family. To my parents, Dennis and Janet, thank you for endowing me with a solid personal compass to work from. I continue to pass the lessons of my childhood on and want both of you to know that you are tremendous people.

Thanks to my sister, Beckie, who has been one of my strongest supporters and cheerleaders. Your optimism and resilience is inspirational!

Thank you to my brother, Danny. While you are no longer here with us, your lessons remain. Primarily, don't judge a book by its cover, respect the individuality in others, and remember that nothing is more important than the intimate bonds of family.

Thank you to my kids—Joey, Emma, Becca, and Megan. You have patiently endured many a weekend afternoon hanging out at home as I wrote (and rewrote) this manuscript. Your innocence, individuality, and unconditional love motivates me every day—to look deeper within myself, to live as an example of the life lessons I want you to embrace, and to continually strive to create an environment that will allow you to live your own best life. You are amazing, and I am so grateful you are in my life!

Finally, I want to thank my best friend, my husband. Jay, I can't imagine what life would be like if I weren't sharing it with you. Your unwavering support, endorsement, and belief are a constant source of strength and courage. Thank you for your acceptance, patience, and encouragement. This book was born on the wings of your love.

FROM THE AUTHOR

The book you hold in your hands is a labor of love—the love of learning, the love of personal transformation, and the love of womankind. When I began writing, my intention was to help women bring joy back into their lives. I saw many of my friends and colleagues living in quiet desperation—focused on getting through the day, juggling work and family obligations, and striving to stay on top of things. Surrounded by the social trappings of personal and professional success, they were struggling to survive.

I understood that applying fundamental coaching principles could help these women take control of their lives. I wanted to give them a chance to stop merely surviving and to start thriving! As I wrote and tested this program with real women, I realized that I was in the midst of a much bigger opportunity than I originally understood. What started as a book to help you live more effectively has turned into an invitation for you to live more passionately and authentically. Essentially, this book has become a call to your spirit.

I have tremendous respect and admiration for you. Though I'm not sure how this program found its way to you, I'm certain that there is a reason it found you. Are you living the life you imagined? Do you like the woman you've become? Will you look back on your life with satisfaction, gratitude, and joy? What does your authentic self want you to do, learn, contribute, or express? I want to help you answer these questions in a way that will cause your heart to overflow.

There is an incredible power within you. In fact, it lives within every woman. Your power will be expressed in a way that is unique to you, and once found it will impact your life and the lives of everyone around you in a profound (and fabulous) way.

Your power may be hidden beneath layers of fear and shame. It may be sleeping, worn-out from trying to get your attention as you run through life. It may be sitting on the sidelines of your heart, uncertain about how the people in your life will respond when it ventures out. No matter how it waits, I promise you it *is* waiting. It wants to be uncovered, awakened, and unleashed.

I wrote this book to help you recognize and rouse your potential, and bring it out into the world. I invite you to embark on this journey with me. It is a process that will call you to re-evaluate many areas of your life. It is a program that will re-energize your sense of purpose, re-establish your natural motivation, and re-ignite your passion. When you finish you will be a true version of yourself, and you will be comfortable in your own skin. What's more, when you look in the mirror you're going to marvel at the magnificence of the woman staring back at you!

Enjoy Your Journey!
Kim

INTRODUCTION

STEP INTO BALANCE

Adrenaline coursed through my veins as I checked the clock on my car's dash for what must have been the seventh time in twenty minutes. My heart was pounding, my breathing shallow, and I could feel the beads of sweat forming on my upper lip. I maneuvered in and out of traffic as if in the Indy 500. I was late and had been all day.

I was beginning to feel that I couldn't maintain a schedule to save my life. I thought of something my grandmother used to say about a woman who lived down the street: "That gal will be late to her own funeral." I shook my head and sighed deeply. I could easily imagine people saying the same about me. I loosened my death grip on the steering wheel and focused on fighting back the tears threatening to spill forth.

The lump in my throat made it difficult to breathe. Fleetingly, I wondered if I might be having a nervous breakdown. A small voice in my head mused that I might get a good night's sleep if I did. Maybe it wasn't such a bad idea.

A child's scream jolted me back to reality. Three of my four children were in the backseat, and the youngest two were engaged in a fierce shouting match. I didn't know what they were fighting over, but I could see they were about to come to blows.

Emma, my oldest, was attempting to change into her soccer gear—while we were moving. I was vaguely aware that I should stop my two younger children from killing each other and that Emma didn't have her seat belt on. I was driving about seventy-five miles per hour, and it occurred to me that I was in the midst of a very bad parenting moment.

I knew that I should pull the car over, allow Emma to change her clothing safely, and democratically mediate the small battle ensuing in the backseat—but I couldn't seem to concentrate. I remembered those wonderful "Calgon, take me away" commercials, which featured frazzled mothers being rescued from the frenzy of their lives and deposited into the calm reverie of a heavenly scented hot bath. I hadn't had a "Calgon Moment" in a very long time.

While I was fully aware of what I should do to care for my children, what I did do was yell at them as I continued to speed down the freeway. I was tired—exhausted really. I didn't have the energy to do the right thing, at least not right then.

I'd been late picking up the girls from school. I was going to be late dropping them off at their respective practices. And I had no idea what I was going to make for dinner. I hadn't made a dent in my to-do list, which was beginning to cover three pages on a yellow legal pad. I remembered thinking earlier in the afternoon that I had at least kept all of the items on one notepad rather than on scraps of paper here and there as I'd done in the past. Under the current circumstances of my life, that was progress. I sighed again—deeply.

That same day, I had plowed through several hundred email messages, made a pitch to a venture capital firm in an attempt to raise a third round of funding for a dot-com company I'd co-founded, and attended several internal meetings to outline company projects that we weren't going to have the money to finance.

I'd left my office late because our management team had called a meeting to discuss our dwindling monies and our lack of real prospects for future funding. It was November 2000, and we had been in business for a year and a half. We had taken more than $20 million in venture capital funding, and we needed at least $10 million more to survive. The economy was crumbling around us. The dot-com industry, which had been so hot and glamorous only a year earlier, had just been dubbed the "dot-bomb" industry, and we were about to become a statistic.

My partners and I had almost 100 employees working diligently to support our business vision, and it was likely that none of them would have jobs in two short months.

But I had to leave our meeting in order to get my kids to soccer practice ...

I made it through the afternoon, managed to get all of my kids to their respective destinations, and put a plausible, albeit take-out, dinner on the table. I'd just sent the girls up for their evening showers when my husband came home. When he asked how my day had been, all I could do was burst into tears.

And so it was, about twenty minutes later, that I found myself sitting on the floor of my laundry room, sobbing hysterically. *Maybe I really am having a nervous breakdown,* I thought. I took a deep breath and attempted to compose myself as I took in the condition of the room around me.

It looked as if a bomb had exploded in it. The marble floors, which I'd been so enthralled with when we built the house, were covered with dirty clothing. There was a half-finished science project sitting on the granite countertop. *We need to make time to finish that over the weekend,* I thought. Next to it were several unwrapped birthday gifts. I made a mental note to buy gift-wrap. I closed my eyes.

I felt empty inside, almost like a zombie. How had my life come to this? It was as if I were living one big to-do list, which by some cruel joke of the universe was destined never to be completed. I was so stretched that I wasn't sure I would ever regain my shape.

I wondered where the happy, passionate, joyful woman I'd once been had disappeared to. "She's buried under your life," my inner voice informed me. Oh no, now I was talking to myself! I frantically shook my head back and forth, further convinced that I was in the midst of an extreme meltdown. I put my head in my hands and took a deep, sustaining breath. *That felt good,* I thought, and took another.

I sat that way for what might have been hours, breathing deeply and thinking about my life. In that time, I considered where I'd come from, took stock of where I was, and decided I wasn't creating a future I wanted to live in. On that evening, sitting on my laundry room floor, dirty socks and towels surrounding me, I realized I'd reached the lowest point I was willing to accept, and I made a decision that changed my life.

THAT WAS THEN, THIS IS NOW

Only a few short years have gone by since then, but that period in my life feels as if it belonged to another woman. And I suppose it did. The decision I made that evening was simple: I committed to getting control of my life. I wanted to feel balanced—I wanted the opportunity to enjoy my marriage, my children, my career, and my home. I decided I wanted to have friends again. And I was determined to bring more Calgon Moments into my life. I wasn't sure how I was going to do it or even whether it could be done, but I knew I had to give it my best shot.

I began with very small steps. I hired a housekeeper and traded carpool duties with another mother. Rather than filling my newly created free time with more items on my to-do list, I started reading self-help books—while in a hot, scented bath.

Eventually, we sold our company, and most of our employees kept their jobs. Our investors got their original capital back, along with a respectable profit. We had become a statistic—a positive one. For that, I was grateful. When our company was absorbed into the larger corporation, I chose to take a new path, and I found the balance that had seemed so elusive just a few short months before.

I took a one-year sabbatical. Though I don't think a sabbatical is required to reclaim control of your life, it was the process I followed. I read more than 100 books that year, completed innumerable personal development programs, and began to connect with myself—perhaps for the first time in my adult life.

Throughout that process, I discovered many things about myself.

I connected with my strengths and passions, and began to research professions that might allow me to apply and integrate them into my life and my work. I found the answer in professional coaching, a relatively new industry that seemed filled with the possibility for business success and the opportunity to help people improve their lives.

BIRTH OF A BLUEPRINT

I decided I wanted to be a coach, and I founded Compass, Inc. I wanted to help women conquer the chaos of today's world and establish life balance. I committed to developing a program that would lead my clients to their version of balanced living in a simple, practical, and profound way.

Over the course of two years, I worked with hundreds of clients, developing the critical steps they could take to define and establish a balanced life. As I worked with each individual, I refined the content of my program, making changes based on what worked and what didn't. After several hundred hours of research and work with clients, I had developed a seven-step program. I was thrilled with the results my clients were getting in their lives, and I was benefiting from applying the principles to my own. I decided it was time to take my program on the road.

I began delivering the course in telephone seminars and group workshops. I was amazed at the response I received. There were huge crowds at every event, and I realized that women were starving for this material. They were exhausted, overscheduled, and burnt-out. They were living in much the same way I had been only a few short years before; it was sobering to discover that the more successful a woman appeared, the more desperately she seemed to need the program.

As a result of taking my work public, I realized I'd hit a nerve. In today's world, with the abundant resources available to us, it's crazy that so many women are leading tired, frazzled, unhappy lives. I knew the program I'd developed could help reverse this problem, so I decided to publish it.

STEPPING INTO BALANCE

The book you hold in your hands has truly been life-tested. It's the result of hundreds of hours of work and client interaction, and it's based on solid methodology from the coaching industry. The seven steps described here have grown and evolved over several years and have benefited from the feedback of many a courageous client. Some of their stories appear in its pages.

FORM AND FUNCTION

The program has seven steps, each covered in its own chapter. The steps are designed to build on one another, so I recommend that you to move through them in order. Of course, if you'd prefer to jump around, you're welcome to do so. If you begin having trouble in any area, you may want to backtrack to earlier portions of the material in order to see what you might have missed. Within each chapter, you'll find four common denominators:

• The Lesson – This gives you the core skills that support the step.

• Client Profiles – Glimpses of my clients' experiences will help you relate to the content and will inspire you to apply it to your own life.

• Call to Action Activities – Information is potential. Applied knowledge is power. The activities in each chapter will help you apply the lessons to your life. These are active exercises. You will complete most of them in a journal, so it's advisable that you designate a notebook or computer file for this purpose. The exercises will help you personalize each lesson, and identify what has to happen for you to establish balance in your life.

• Key Learning Points – Each chapter ends with a summary of its core lessons.

LIFE ON YOUR TERMS

It's likely you picked up this book because you're burnt-out, exhausted, frustrated, and tired of juggling your way through life. Say goodbye to this frazzled version of yourself, because once you commit to the seven-step program, your life will change. With this program, you will:

- align your energy with your priorities and begin managing your time more effectively
- stop juggling the demands of others, start saying *no*, and communicate more effectively
- clearly identify your priorities, and learn to make decisions based on what's important to you
- understand why you do what you do, and stop doing what you no longer want to do
- uncover your individual strengths, unleash your natural enthusiasm, and reach for your potential
- define what you want in your life and career, and go for it
- reconnect with what you stand for, and like who you are
- change behaviors that don't serve you, and condition yourself to those that do
- develop strong, intimate, dynamic relationships
- fall in love with your life, feel like a kid again, and get excited about waking up in the morning
- live in balance

Three factors will be critical to your success. The first requires you to make time to read this book and apply the seven steps to your life. The second involves your willingness to define your version of balance. The third calls for you to set yourself up for success.

MAKING THE TIME

I recommend that you read the book first without doing any of the activities. Once you've completed your reading, begin to move through the program one step at a time, allowing yourself as little as one week or as much as one month for each step.

If you're part of the "right now" generation, you may recoil at the suggestion that this program could take as long as seven months to complete. Real change happens gradually. It isn't something you check off your to-do list. I would guess that it took you many years, possibly decades, to create the chaos you're currently living in. A commitment of seven weeks or even seven months to get control and create lasting change should be small in comparison.

Invariably, when life's demands increase, the first thing that decreases is the time we make available to ourselves, which is the very thing we need most to successfully meet our responsibilities. It's time to decide that you're going to begin taking care of yourself again. Your first commitment must be to make the time to work this program.

YOUR DEFINITION OF BALANCE

You are unique, and your life is like no other. What equates to life balance for your neighbor or co-worker probably won't work for you. You must define *balance* for yourself.

Throughout the program, I will walk you through activities designed to help you personalize the seven steps. It will be crucial for you to move through these activities authentically and honestly. The definition your community, corporation, family, or church gives to *balance* is not the one you need to work with. You will succeed when you reach deep within yourself and create a balance blueprint that is completely personal to you.

Balance isn't necessarily about not being busy, although that may be part of your definition. It's about taking care of all of you and all of what is important to you. Your path will require you to define who you are and what matters to you, uncover your strengths, identify your passions, acknowledge your fears, and embrace your dreams. As you define the "what" of balance, the "how" will reveal itself. As you begin making the changes required to support your new equilibrium, you will re-engage with your life force, and what once seemed unattainable will be part of your daily experience.

SETTING YOURSELF UP TO WIN

You may encounter a few stumbling blocks on the road to balance. The two that most of my clients seem to need help with have to do with anticipating obstacles and creating support systems.

Anticipating Obstacles

Have you ever embarked on a personal development program only to fall off the wagon within a few weeks of getting started? What caused you to fail?

Did you have trouble making the time to apply the program's material? Did you try to do too much at once? Were you talking to yourself in a disempowering way, saying things such as, "I never finish what I start" or "It won't matter anyway"?

Invest a few moments to identify the one or two key things you know could stop you from successfully completing this program. Once you've determined what they are, decide how you'll handle them, and handle them before you get started.

For example, if you've failed in the past because you didn't have time to work through the material in a program, sit down with your calendar and make appointments with yourself for the next eight months. Give yourself one month to read the book and another seven months to apply the material to your life. I know this seems like a long time, but keep this in mind: In eight months, your life can be better than it is right now, or it can be worse. You get to decide which.

If you've discovered that you talk to yourself in a self-defeating manner, decide that you are going to stop. It's really that simple. Instead of telling yourself, "I never finish what I start," change that phrase to "I may not have finished programs in the past, but I'm not living in the past. I'm living in the present, and right now I'm committed to finishing this program."

If, in the past, you've bitten off more than you could chew and that caused you to feel overwhelmed and to quit, you are a prime candidate for taking the full eight months to complete this program. Remember, we're looking to create long-term change. Set achievable goals for yourself so that you have a chance to win.

Securing a Support System

The seven-step process within this book is simple, meaning it's easy to understand, but it won't be easy. Long-held habits and behaviors can be difficult to change. Altering them requires consistency and focus. Your ability to show up for yourself each day will be crucial to your success. The support of another person can help you celebrate your wins and push you through the rough spots. You can secure support in different ways.

• *Hire a Coach.* I highly recommend hiring a professional coach to support you in this process. The structure and encouragement a great coach provides can be invaluable in you reaching your goals. While it can be very expensive to work with a professional coach privately, it has become my mission to make coaching accessible and affordable. In fact, I am so committed to making sure that every woman has access to affordable coaching that I founded a company to provide this type of service. At *www.mylifecompass.com*, you can work with a professionally trained coach who specializes in this material for as little as $39 per month! Visit *www.mylifecompass.com* to find out more.

• *Use the Buddy System.* Enlist the support of a close friend or family member. This person should be someone you trust and know will follow through. Agree on the pace you'll use to move through the material, how frequently you'll meet, and how much information you'd like to share with each other.

• *Start a Group.* Form a group of like-minded individuals who are committed to moving through the program together, or visit *www.mylifecompass.com* to find an existing coaching group, led by a professionally trained Compass Coach, you can join.

Regardless of the form your support system takes, please put one in place. We all need a shoulder to lean on every once in a while. Make sure you have some strong ones available to support you as you embark on this journey.

LET'S GET STARTED

Like a tree, you need a solid root system to support your growth. As you move through the seven steps, you'll establish both a personal foundation and a life system, and you'll begin to develop a natural balance to support your life and work.

You may never have thought about some of the things I'll ask you to consider, and you may prefer not to follow through on some of the things I'll ask you to do. Please remember that you cannot change what you do not acknowledge. However, once you consider a new perspective and acknowledge what isn't working, you'll be amazed at the powerful resources you discover within and around you, just waiting to support you in changing your reality.

I believe there is a higher order in our world, and it moves in to support you when you decide you're ready to ask for more. Be real and honest with yourself as you move through this program. Make the time to take inventory. Be willing to look at what's working and what isn't. And, again, have the courage to tell the truth.

A final word: You always have a choice. You've created your present reality, and you're capable of manifesting a new one. You're not a victim of circumstance. On the contrary, you're a powerful woman and you can make your wildest dreams come true.

The *Remodel Your Reality* process requires some elbow grease, but I have to believe you're ready—because this book found you. Now, commit to finding yourself and the fulfillment that lives on the other side of your discovery.

PART

ONE

MANAGE YOUR
ENERGY

RECLAIM YOUR ENERGY: THE THREE FACTORS OF VITALITY

A disheveled woman raced into my office, breathing hard. Her words tumbled out: "I'm so sorry I'm late. I didn't leave the office on time to pick up my daughter from school. She was upset with me, so I had to stop and calm her down before I dropped her off at ballet. I couldn't call to let you know I was running behind because my cell-phone battery died." She sighed, and slumped in the chair across from my desk. Glancing at her watch, she added, "I have to be back in my office in about an hour, so we should probably get to it."

This high-powered Silicon Valley executive, who had a reputation for being tough as nails, looked anything but tough now as she tried to compose herself for what was only her second appointment with me. She'd been late for our first meeting as well, having arrived in a similar frenzy. She had hired me to help her create balance in her life. I could see that we had some serious work to do.

I said, "It sounds like you've had a chaotic afternoon."

Her breathing had slowed, and she'd reached a point of composure. But her skin was ashen, and there were dark circles under her eyes. She smiled wanly and replied, "Really, it's more like I'm living in chaos every day. It just doesn't seem to end." She stopped for a moment and rubbed her temples. "I don't think I can keep up this pace much longer. I feel like I'm running full tilt on a treadmill, but I'm not getting anywhere. Last week we talked about the possibility of creating a fulfilling life, but I can't seem to focus on anything other than surviving from one day to the next."

"Well," I said quietly, "what are you willing to do to change that?"

Her head popped up, and we locked gazes. For the first time, I saw a slight twinkle in her eyes as she said, "That's why I'm here."

STEP OFF THE TREADMILL

It's a good possibility that you purchased this book because you relate to this woman and you want help! You may feel overtired, over-scheduled, and overwhelmed. Like many of the women I've worked with in my coaching practice, it's likely you're juggling multiple responsibilities and struggling to manage the many tasks required by both your work and home lives. I would guess that it isn't unusual for you to fall into bed at the end of the night, exhausted, realizing that the only person you didn't take care of throughout the day was yourself.

How many times have you decided you were going to start a new hobby, such as taking dance lessons, or begin a new exercise routine, only to put these commitments at the bottom of your list when something more "urgent" came up? How many times have you cancelled plans to connect with your girlfriends because someone at the office needed your help with a last-minute project? How many times have you waited to use the bathroom, thinking you could handle "just one more task" before you took the three minutes required to relieve yourself?

How on earth do I know these things? Very simply put—I am a woman, and I've walked in your shoes. I have four children, two households, a dog, horses, and my own business. Believe me, I understand the demands of a busy life. I also know these things because I'm a professional coach who works with women every day. I help my clients reconnect with themselves, reclaim their energy, and remodel their realities. Together, we create the results they want in their lives and businesses.

My work has afforded me the opportunity to understand the common challenges women face. I've seen many talented, strong, brilliant women drowning in their lives. Thankfully, I've helped almost as many learn to swim in those swirling waters.

I'd like to be your coach, and help you create the life of your dreams. I invite you to use the program in this book to do just that. The tools and strategies we'll discuss are designed to help you take control of every aspect of your life and work. As you move through each step, your reality will change and you will change. You will learn to communicate clearly. You will identify what you *really* want versus what you believe you *should* want. You will manage your time more effectively, you will take charge of your behavior, and you will have more satisfying relationships. Ultimately, you will be a truer version of yourself. In the first step of our program, we're going to reclaim your energy.

ENERGY ACCOUNTING

I have yet to work with a client who begins her personal journey by committing to managing her energy. Normally, people like to begin their development process by setting goals and strategizing. While great value can be derived from these activities, even people with strong determination will falter along their path if they have not first secured the well of energy required to process new ideas, opportunities, and perspectives.

Energy is the physical and mental power to perform work. You require energy to support every thought, word, action, and interaction in your life. The cruel joke relative to energy is that you're only given a finite portion of it each day.

Let's imagine that you're allotted 100 units of energy every morning. Whether you do it consciously or unconsciously, you invest those units throughout the day. Waking up in the morning, under ideal circumstances, might require 10 units. Dropping the kids off at school and commuting to your office could require 15 more. Greeting co-workers, checking voicemail and email, and moving through your morning schedule might cost you 20 more units, and so on. As you engage in the many responsibilities of your life and work, your 100 units of energy are allocated.

This formula works beautifully, assuming your circumstances are ideal. But ideal circumstances are rare. Multiple factors impact your environment, many of which you have no control over. You cannot evade morning traffic, it's not possible to stop your insufferable co-worker from being a creep, and it's unlikely you're going to impede the incessant flow of email to your in-box.

These annoyances increase the "cost" of your normal daily activities. If your house is a mess and you can't find the items you're looking for in the morning, getting up and out of the house might cost you 20 units instead of 10. If you leave late and the morning traffic becomes not only an annoyance but also a circumstance of your being later, the stress involved in that situation could ratchet what should have cost you 15 units to more than 30. If you haven't let your co-worker know what form of communication you will tolerate from him, his creepiness could cost you still more. Ultimately, once you've allocated enough of your energy to these cost increases, you begin to operate within an energy deficit.

How do you know if you're operating in an energy deficit? If you feel fatigued throughout the day, it's possible you are. If you wake up tired after a full-night's rest, it's probable you are. If this sounds familiar, then it's time for an energy makeover! It's time for you to employ strategies that increase your energy reserves and apply tactics that address those areas that are draining you.

THE THREE FACTORS OF VITALITY

There are three kinds of energy—physical, mental, and emotional. The way you manage these areas will impact your ability to live each day with vitality. As we consider the three factors, I challenge you to identify places in your life where you can increase the energy available to you.

PHYSICAL ENERGY

The physical factor of energy involves your physiological body and your material environment. The manner in which you care for your physical world directly impacts the energy available to you each day. Ultimately, these elements have the opportunity to support and simplify your life or to create repetitive stress and complexity in your daily experience.

Think about how much time you waste each day looking for your keys, changing clothing because you can't find items that match one another, or sorting through unmanageable stacks of mail and paperwork. What else could you do with that time? How many times have you started your morning running around in a frenzied state because you'd hit the snooze button one too many times, and the alarm had turned itself off? How much more pleasant could each day be if your physical surroundings supported your personal rhythm and routine and if you had so much physical energy that you were able to get out of bed the *first* time your alarm rang?

This is possible, and it all begins with your commitment to take control of your physical surroundings.

CALL TO ACTION – ASSESS YOUR PHYSICAL ENERGY

Take the following energy assessment, which is designed to help you identify where you may be losing physical power. Answer either *yes* or *no* to each question.

HOME ENVIRONMENT

1. Is your home clean?
2. Have you defined a list of regular cleaning duties to support maintenance of your home, and then assigned those duties to responsible partners?

3. Does every item you own have a home, or a place where it belongs?
4. Do you use or need every item you own?
5. Are the items you own in good condition and working order?
6. Does your home décor feel like a reflection of you?
7. Do you have a special place in your house where you can go to relax and unwind?
8. Is your car in good condition? Is it serviced regularly, is it clean, and does it function as a reliable form of transportation?
9. Is all of your clothing in good condition and of the right size?

WORK ENVIRONMENT

1. Do you have a filing system to support the information you need to manage?
2. Do you have a system for managing incoming communication?
3. Do you handle each document only once, acting on it, filing it, or tossing it as it crosses your path?
4. Do you have a system for tracking and managing due dates?
5. Do you have on hand the supplies you need to work effectively?
6. Is your environment clean and neat? Can you see your desktop?
7. Have you personalized your environment? Do you have photos, plants, or music that support(s) you in feeling at home and peaceful while you work?
8. Do you delete or file email messages once you've responded to them?
9. Do you throw out or file documents related to completed projects or projects that have been put on hold?

PHYSIOLOGICAL CARE

1. Are you happy with your body weight?
2. Do you eat 5–6 meals and snacks throughout the day?
3. Do you eat a nutritious, well-balanced diet?
4. Do you drink 8–10 glasses of water each day?
5. Do you get 7–9 hours of sleep each night?
6. Do you engage in some form of exercise at least 5 days per week?
7. Do you like your physical appearance?
8. Do you see your doctor and dentist for regular checkups?
9. Do you have a skincare routine that supports healthy skin?

Any question you answered *no* to is very likely contributing to your energy deficit. It's important to understand what isn't working. Until you can see this clearly, you cannot make a change. Once you realize where you are losing energy, you can begin to take it back.

Strategies to Manage Your Material Environment

When you proactively commit to managing your environment, you not only reduce the energy cost of routine tasks, you also increase your personal comfort and satisfaction. Whether you realize it or not, your surroundings have a strong impact on you. A chaotic, disorganized setting is energetically expensive. While it may require some elbow grease up front, creating a well-ordered environment at work and at home will increase your vitality.

I use four strategies when I embark on this process with my clients. I encourage you to apply these strategies to your physical space, and feel the satisfying surge of strength and power that accompanies your commitment.

Clear Your Space

It may seem counterproductive to invest energy in cleaning up your environment. After all, you want to increase your power, not engage in the drudgery of cleaning closets or sorting files. However, a clean, orderly environment is imperative if your goal is to maintain high levels of energy.

You can approach this task in a number of ways. It may make sense for you to set a weekend aside and move through your home room by room, discarding damaged items, donating things you no longer need or use, and sorting items you'd like to keep. Once you've moved through each item in a room, clean the space thoroughly.

After you've tackled each room in your home, take inventory of any projects you may need to manage, such as door repairs, paint touch-ups, or carpet cleaning. Then, begin to work through this list one item at a time.

Use this same approach at the office, moving drawer to drawer instead of room to room. Discard files you no longer need, delegate projects that have been collecting dust, and thoroughly clean your desks and credenzas. You may even want to add a plant or photo to remind you of your commitment to increase your vitality.

While initially daunting, this process can be very satisfying because it provides you with almost immediate gratification. After just a few days of focused action, your home and work environments will embrace you with their cleanliness and order, and you'll feel satisfied that you invested in the task.

Find a Home for Every Item

It is much easier to maintain order in your environment when every item has a home or a place where it belongs. As you move through the room-to-room sweep of your home and drawer-to-drawer sweep of your office, make sure to decide where you will keep each of the things you're hanging on to.

It's helpful to group similar items together, placing things close to where you're likely to use them. For example, healthy snacks can be kept in a selected drawer at your office, and magazines can be grouped in a basket by your favorite chair at home.

Once you've selected a home for your possessions, keep them where they belong. After you're through using something, make sure you place it back in its home. This way, you'll always know where to find what you're looking for, and the order you so painstakingly restored will be maintained.

Ownership Is Everything

Running a home is a monumental task, especially if there are other people (for example, little people) in your family. I established a rule in our home a long time ago that I would not do things for my children that they could do for themselves. As a result, they put their own laundry away. They clear their plates from the table and put them in the dishwasher. When they take something out, such as a toy or book, they are responsible to put the item back when they're finished with it. They've been successfully following these standards since they were as young as four years old. Admittedly, I'm still working on my husband, but that's another story.

It will be so much easier to maintain order in your home if you clearly set and communicate standards that require your family to work as a team. Your roles may include mother and wife, but they don't need to include maid. Call a family meeting, and make sure everyone is clear about what will be required of him or her to maintain your newly established order. Then, hold each of them to those expectations.

Not only is it acceptable to ask each member of your household to pick up after himself or herself, it's also plausible to delegate routine tasks such as loading the dishwasher, gathering the laundry, and running the vacuum. Make sure that you ask for, and allow yourself to receive, help in the management of your home.

Outsource It

In business, outsourcing involves hiring an outside party to manage an operational process on your behalf. This principle can support you in managing the many tasks associated with your life as well. If the prospect of organizing every room in your home or each space in your office is too distasteful to contemplate, hire a professional organizer to take over the task. If cooking dinner after a full workday feels cumbersome, embrace the concept of take-out or hire a cook to prepare a week's worth of meals for your family. Ask your assistant to take over your filing or to return phone calls on your behalf.

This strategy need not require a huge financial investment. Many times, support professionals work at moderate hourly rates. If you don't have the wiggle room in your budget to hire someone, it's possible to establish a trade relationship with a friend or neighbor. The point is to get clear about the things you don't want to do, or those you're confident you will successfully avoid doing, and find someone to help you accomplish the necessary tasks.

There is no shame in asking for help. Feel free to proactively seek opportunities to delegate tasks you'd prefer not to invest in, and embrace those you most enjoy.

Strategies for Your Physiological Body

The link between energy and your physical body is obvious. If you take great care of your health, you will feel more vital and vigorous. If you don't, you may feel lethargic and fatigued. When you make a commitment to embrace the simple strategies I'm about to share with you, you will experience a profound increase in your energy in as little as a few days.

Establish a Hydration Habit

Fluid is a magic elixir. Your body is ⅔ water and must maintain adequate fluid levels to control its temperature, aid digestive processes, and support the production of energy molecules. Dehydration, which is brought on by a lack of fluid in the diet, is one of the leading causes of fatigue.

It seems simple, and it is. A very easy way for you to increase your energy level is to make sure you're hydrating your body. Generally accepted guidelines recommend active women drink between eight and eleven 8-ounce glasses of fluid each day.

One easy way to address your body's fluid needs involves drinking water throughout the day. Another suggests you incorporate water-rich foods, such as fruits and vegetables, into your diet. I recommend that my clients begin the day with a glass of water, accompany each meal with a cool drink, and carry a water bottle around with them. You may want to apply a similar approach.

If you don't like the taste of plain water, try flavored waters, which are sold in your grocery and convenience stores, or herbal iced tea. You can also try adding sliced lemon, lime, or cucumbers to a pitcher of water to create a clean and refreshing drink.

Establish a hydration habit! This may be the easiest and most efficient strategy you apply to increase your level of physical vigor.

Eat Well and Often

This is not an invitation to go on a diet, and this isn't a diet book. It is a challenge to make sure you're fueling your body throughout the day. Essentially, food is fuel, and you need to eat every four to five hours to keep your body supplied with energy.

The quality of the food you eat also factors into the energy equation. It's important to nourish yourself each time you eat. This is most effectively accomplished when you include fruits, vegetables, whole grains, and lean proteins in each meal.

Essentially, your energetic furnace will be most efficiently stoked if you feed it a combination of protein, complex carbohydrate, and fat every time you eat. Protein is the building block of muscle. It maintains cells, transports hormones and vitamins, and helps to regulate the release of energy. Protein sources include meat, eggs, poultry, fish, nuts, beans, soy products, and low-fat dairy products.

Carbohydrates have taken a pretty good beating in the last couple of years, but they are the body's preferred source of energy. While heavily processed starches are not supportive of sustained energy management, complex carbohydrates and simple carbohydrates found in their natural state can be powerful contributors to your vitality.

Processed carbohydrates—which include white bread, white rice, sugar-laden sweets, and most pre-packaged foods—may give you a rapid kick in energy, but that kick will be short-lived. This can be largely attributed to the lack of fiber found in most processed foods, which ultimately impacts your blood sugar in a negative way.

Complex carbohydrates, on the other hand, sustain blood sugar levels, which supports you in maintaining high levels of energy. Complex carbohydrates include whole grains and starchy vegetables, such as potatoes, sweet potatoes, and carrots.

Simple carbohydrates found in their natural state include fruits and non-starchy vegetables. These foods provide you with a multitude of vitamins, a high level of fluid, and a healthy dose of fiber, which helps your body's furnace burn more steadily.

Fat, which has also taken a hit from the diet industry, can be an invaluable tool in helping you to feel satisfied with fewer calories. Including small portions of polyunsaturated fats—found in seafood and vegetable oils—and monounsaturated fats—found in meat, poultry, nuts, and olive oil—can help you manage your appetite, allowing your body to function at a high level energetically.

Begin each morning with a balanced breakfast, incorporating protein, carbohydrates, and fat. Fuel your body every four to five hours with another balanced meal or snack, and enjoy the sustained release of energy you experience throughout the day.

Slide into Sleep

This strategy is simple yet not easy. It's simple in that it's obvious that you need adequate sleep to ensure high levels of energy. It isn't easy, because you have to manage your behavior (and your busy schedule) to make this strategy work for you.

Lack of sleep has been proven to reduce levels of concentration, increase irritability, and provoke monster sugar cravings. Translated, lack of sleep makes you less fun to be around, less productive after everyone has run away from your sleep-deprived persona, and more prone to inhale a pint of Ben and Jerry's instead of working on that project you've committed yourself to.

Individual needs for sleep vary, but general guidelines recommend between seven and nine hours of shut-eye each night. If you're among the many women who has to be up by 6:00 a.m. in order to get a jump on your day, that means you need to be in bed before midnight.

Initially, you may need to experiment with the amount of sleep you require. When I'm working with a client, we usually get started with a goal of seven hours per night, because that is typically the most manageable place to begin. Then, we monitor how she is feeling each week and increase her sleep-time if she feels she needs more. You many want to try a similar approach.

The only way to make sure you get enough sleep is to decide you're going to get to bed each night at a time that allows you to get the number of hours you need. If you need seven hours of sleep and have to be up at 6:00 a.m., decide you'll be in bed by 11:00 p.m. That means that whatever doesn't get done by that time at night must wait until the next day.

Again, this is simple yet not easy. We'll be diving into some effective time management strategies in a later step. For now, realize that you're in charge of your sleep schedule, and make sure that you get the rest you need.

Exercise

Investing time in exercise will produce massive gains in your energy level. An activity as simple as walking generates enormous physiological benefits, which result in higher levels of vitality and feelings of wellness.

Make ten minutes in your day to incorporate stretching exercises, or find a colleague who'd like to take a lunch-hour walk. By getting to bed early enough, you may be able to carve out twenty to thirty minutes in the morning for an exercise video, or you could decide you'll start going straight from the office to the gym.

No matter what activity you commit to, approach your decision with the intent to create a reservoir of energy. This reserve will support you during hectic and chaotic times. While smaller thighs are a nice side effect, the point is to take great care of yourself and generate the energy you need to see you through your life and work.

Wrapping It Up

The more willing you are to invest in managing your material environment and your physiological body, the more likely you are to experience high levels of energy in your day-to-day reality. As I've said, the strategies we've covered are simple yet not always easy. They become possible when you commit to them.

CLIENT PROFILE – MARY

Mary was a vivacious woman in her late forties. She was the mother of four children between the ages of six and sixteen. She owned and operated an interior design firm and volunteered for a local non-profit organization. She came to see me because she had reached the end of her rope. She was exhausted, burnt-out, and not sure where to begin.

After moving through our initial interview, it became clear to me that Mary was living in a managed state of chaos. Her beautiful home was in disarray, and her description of the family's weekly schedule was sobering to say the least. She was averaging five hours of sleep per night and eating erratically, usually driving through a fast-food restaurant or ordering take-out due to a lack of time.

The first thing we looked at was how Mary was caring for herself. In essence, she wasn't. Certainly, she took a shower and put on her makeup every morning, but she wasn't nourishing her body, getting enough sleep, or making time for exercise. In our first two weeks of working together I challenged Mary to make three specific changes.

First, we determined that she had to get up at 6:00 a.m. each morning. I challenged her to be in bed with the lights off by 11:00 p.m. each night. We set a rule that whatever task she hadn't completed by 10:30 p.m. would be transitioned into the next day's calendar. At 10:30 p.m. she would retire to her bedroom and take a hot bath or watch the evening news. At 11:00 p.m. she would turn the lights off.

My second challenge for Mary was for her to drink one full glass of water as soon as she woke up, and another every two hours throughout the day.

Her third assignment was to eat something every three hours. We established a list of healthy snacks, and she was on her way. Two weeks later Mary was on top of the world. She had enjoyed a full night's rest for the first time in years and had been surprised at how much drinking water and eating regularly had increased her energy throughout the day. She was ready to move into our next phase.

We took a look at the family's weekly schedule and made a list of the routine tasks that had to be addressed each month. I advised Mary to call a family meeting, where she would ask each member of her clan to take ownership of specific tasks and establish a daily routine based on their typically scheduled activities. Her final assignment involved committing two full weekends to tackle the family home and enlisting the help of every member of her family for the project—even her six-year-old daughter.

After working with me for only two months, Mary had taken control of the physical component of her energy. She had cleaned up her surroundings, started taking care of her body, and established a schedule that helped her family function more effectively.

Mary's willingness to improve the care she was giving herself and to take control of her surroundings helped her free energy that could then be focused on more important tasks. In fact, in our third month of working together she had so much additional energy that we were able to shift our focus to the task of developing more business for her now-booming interior decorating firm.

CALL TO ACTION – INCREASE YOUR PHYSICAL ENERGY

This activity will help you establish a starting point for your energy makeover. Keep in mind that you don't need to employ all of the strategies outlined in this section or address every item identified in your energy assessment to successfully increase your energy. Small changes will provide you with an expanded sense of vitality. Identify the items you believe will have the greatest impact on your day-to-day reality, and get started with those.

• Set a weekend aside to tackle your material environment. If you believe the job will take longer to complete, decide which rooms you'll address in the amount of time you're able to schedule. Take action during your committed time, using the strategies in this chapter, and notice the increase in your energy level.

• Select one of the strategies we reviewed to support your physiological body. For two weeks, focus on incorporating this strategy into your life. At the beginning of Week Three, pick a second strategy to begin including in your schedule. Every third week, incorporate another strategy, until you're successfully using them all.

Enjoy your increasing levels of energy!

MENTAL ENERGY

Your energy is impacted by what goes on in your head. You can liken the available space in your mind to that of a computer's hard drive. The more items you save in your memory bank, the less space you have available to support your vitality. While factors in this area are slightly less tangible than those impacting your physical energy, they are no less profound.

Mental energy revolves around your commitments. When you maintain an inventory of projects you've started but not finished, a running to-do list, or a series of cumbersome promises, you set yourself up for energetic depletion, because each of these items takes up valuable space in your mind.

CALL TO ACTION – ASSESS YOUR MENTAL ENERGY

Take the following energy assessment, which is designed to help you identify where you may be losing mental power. Answer either *yes* or *no* to each question.

1. Do you schedule more tasks in a given day than you can reasonably accomplish?
2. Do you put important tasks or projects off?
3. Do you have a list of half-completed projects that need to be addressed?
4. Are you consistently late to scheduled appointments?

5. Do you accept requests and invitations you would prefer to decline?
6. Do you spend time with people you don't like?
7. Do you commit to projects out of a sense of obligation?
8. Do you accept responsibilities because you're worried about what others will think of you if you don't?
9. Have the same tasks or projects been on your to-do list for more than three months?

Any question you answered *yes* to is very likely contributing to your energy deficit. Again, your willingness to honestly assess what isn't working will help you make corrections where they're needed. The following strategies will help you do just that.

Strategies to Manage Your Mental Energy

Making commitments you fail to make good on undermines your self-esteem and diminishes your confidence in your ability to follow through. In our second step, we'll talk about how to make decisions about what you commit to. Before we do that, let's identify and clear the items you currently have stored in your mental hard drive.

Tame Your To-Do List

I'm convinced that all women will reach the end of their lives with a to-do list. You juggle so many roles and responsibilities in your daily life, how could you function without one? Used proactively, lists can be great tools for supporting you in tracking the actions you need to take. Used destructively, lists can create feelings of overwhelm, frustration, and defeat.

The most common mistake I've encountered with the use of the "to-do list" involves overestimating what can actually be accomplished in one day. Attempting to complete twenty tasks in a day, in and around the other responsibilities of your life and work, is a sure recipe for feeling like a failure. In many instances, Superwoman couldn't complete the lists some of my clients have shared with me.

I use two strategies when working with my clients to tame their lists. The first puts some structure to your activities, making them easier to manage. The second sets you up for success.

Structure Your Tasks

Invest a few moments to write down every to-do you currently have floating around in your head. Once you've completed this step, review each item on your list and ask yourself if the item in question really needs to be completed.

I've worked with many clients who took such satisfaction in crossing things off their list or who got such a charge from having a full list of things to do that they put items on their lists that really didn't need to be addressed. Evaluate your inventory, and make sure that each task you've noted really needs to be handled.

Once you've cleared any tasks that don't need addressing, group related activities into categories. For example, all tasks that involve running errands could be organized into one category, items that require phone calls another, and so on. Once you've created your categories, you may want to identify those things that are repetitive, such as going to the grocery store or the bank, and those that are occasional, such as buying an item at the hardware store.

An effective way to manage repetitive activities is to establish a routine around their completion. Is it possible for you to create a standard list of groceries and have them delivered to your home on a schedule that suits you? If you live in an urban or suburban area, there are many Internet grocers who now provide this type of service. Is it possible for you to have your dry cleaner deliver to your home, instead of your having to make the trip to their store each week? Investing a small amount of time to set up a system that supports your repetitive errands can simplify your process.

When addressing occasional errands, it's most productive to group them together and attempt to complete them within close proximity to one another. While this is not always possible, your willingness to consider this new approach can support you in managing your inventory of tasks.

Set Yourself Up for Success

The most certain way to free your mental energy from the burden of to-dos is to take effective action. Commit to acting on a set number of items each day and you will create a momentum that supports you in addressing the tasks currently on your list as well as new ones that arise each day.

I advise my clients to commit to no more than ten tasks a day. At the beginning of each day, identify the three most critical things that need to be addressed. Get started with those and methodically move through the other items on your list as the day progresses. If you're not able to get to everything, just transfer the pending activities to your calendar in the next few days.

The most important factors in taming your to-do list involve getting your tasks out of your head and deciding that you will act on the list you've created in a consistent and achievable manner. When you employ these strategies, you will experience a positive shift in your energy and a sense of satisfaction related to your progress.

Take a Project Inventory

Management of projects is very similar to that of to-dos. It's quite common to have an inventory of uncompleted plans in your mind. A project is something you'd like to create or accomplish that requires multiple steps. For example, drafting a financial plan and redecorating a room are projects.

Take inventory of the unfinished projects in your mind. Get them on paper and evaluate them to determine if they're still meaningful to you. If they're not, give yourself permission to put them to rest. You have a right to change your mind! If they are, get clear about what you want the outcome of each project to be—for example, a completed financial plan—and decide why this end result is important to you. Meaning creates momentum, so the process of connecting with why you'd like to accomplish the goal at hand will energize your actions.

Once you've identified those projects you're committed to, prioritize them. Decide which you'll do first, second, and so on. Then, begin working through the steps you'll need to take to act on your first priority. Decide to commit a specific amount of time to the completion of your enterprise each week and follow through on that commitment. Work on one project at a time, giving yourself permission to move slowly and steadily.

The simple act of getting your projects out of your head, sorting through those you are committed to versus those that no longer make sense for you, and prioritizing what remains can be incredibly liberating. Couple that with committed, consistent action and your energy level will begin to soar.

Stop "Shoulding" on Yourself

I cannot count the number of times I've worked with a client who was managing a list of commitments she'd made as a result of feeling that she "should" do so. This is a sure way to diminish your energy levels and undermine your ability to enjoy life.

When you commit yourself to an activity out of a sense of obligation, you are setting yourself up to feel overwhelmed, resentful, and possibly even angry. Living your life according to someone else's expectations will put you on a path to unhappiness and regret.

Make sure you only lend your time and energy to tasks and projects that are meaningful to you. If you're asked to participate in something you'd rather not be involved in, say *no*. While this may be uncomfortable in the moment, it will save you many hours of frustration and regret in the future. It will also free up a wellspring of energy!

Take a moment to list every commitment you're currently involved in. Evaluate the quality of each obligation. Did you agree to participate in the endeavor because it was meaningful to you, or did you agree because you felt you should?

If you agreed to a commitment out of a sense of obligation, consider the possibility of withdrawing from that undertaking. Clearing the "shoulds" from your life will very likely lift a weight off your shoulders and infuse you with newfound vitality.

Wrapping It Up

While slightly intangible, the items impacting your mental energy are not difficult to manage. When applied, these strategies can help you take control of many of the cumbersome requirements of your life in a manner that supports and empowers you. When you decide to reclaim your energy using any of these methods, you will benefit from a surge of renewal and energetic restoration.

CALL TO ACTION – INCREASE YOUR MENTAL ENERGY

This activity is designed to address the mental component of your energy makeover. Again, you do not have to implement all of the mental management strategies or address all of the items from the mental energy assessment in order to increase your power. Real change happens gradually, so identify the items you believe will make the most impact in your life and begin your process by addressing those.

• Write down every to-do in your mental inventory. Separate the tasks that really need to be completed from those that do not. Then, prioritize the remaining items on your list.

• Identify the tasks or responsibilities you routinely manage and determine which can be grouped together, such as errands to run or calls to make, and which could be automated, such as weekly grocery or dry-cleaning deliveries.

- Move through a similar process with your projects. Summarize all pending objectives, separate the projects you really need to accomplish versus those you don't, and prioritize those that remain.
- Once you've sorted through your to-do list and your project inventory, decide on a limit to the number of tasks you will attempt each day and commit to only one project at a time. Allow yourself to take small steps each day, and enjoy the sense of accomplishment that accompanies the surge of personal power you feel!

EMOTIONAL ENERGY

The emotional factors of energy are usually the most challenging to deal with. These have to do with life experiences that are unresolved and are directly linked to your interactions with other people. They can be charged with angst—such as feelings of guilt, shame, fear, embarrassment, frustration, anger, and regret.

CALL TO ACTION – ASSESS YOUR EMOTIONAL ENERGY

Take the following assessment, designed to help you identify where you may be losing emotional energy. Answer either *yes* or *no* to each question.

1. Do you tell the truth, even when it's uncomfortable to do so?
2. Do you say *no* to invitations you aren't interested in accepting?
3. Do you spend time only with people you like and enjoy?
4. Do you require the people in your life to treat you with respect?
5. Do you feel loved and accepted by those closest to you?
6. Have you accepted the experiences in your past?
7. Have you let go of any past anger or regret?

8. Are you able to ask for what you want?

9. Are your current relationships clean and constructive?

Any question you answered *no* to is very likely contributing to your energy deficit. These are more complex issues than those within your physical or mental inventories. For that reason, you may need to approach them more slowly, carefully, and thoughtfully. The next strategies will help you do just that.

Strategies to Manage Your Emotional Energy

There are four primary situations that impact your emotional energy. Invariably, you will identify with each scenario to some degree. Inevitably, each of us has experienced distressful and dissatisfying interactions with others, and most of us have been disappointed in our own behavior at one time or another.

Experiences that impact your emotions only diminish your energy when they're left unresolved. The best way to determine if a situation is unresolved is to connect with the charge of feeling you have associated with the experience. If you can recall the scenario with a level of neutrality and calm, it's probable that you've reached a level of closure related to that event. It's even possible you've pulled valuable lessons from your encounter.

If, however, you feel a jolt of emotion, such as anger, fear, shame, embarrassment, or regret when recalling the event, it's likely you have some unresolved feelings to contend with. These are the experiences that use precious units of your energy and that you need to inventory.

Your Own Actions

If you have done something that violates your sense of right and wrong, you may feel incomplete. If this action caused harm to another person, you will almost certainly feel incomplete. The actions in this area vary from person to person, as everyone has a different set of rules that govern his or her behavior. Examples of these actions can range in seriousness from something as seemingly harmless as failing to keep a commitment, to more serious offenses such as telling a lie or gossiping about a friend or family member.

Take inventory of your personal behavior. Do you have regrets about anything you've said or done that you may need to address? Do you owe anyone an apology? If so, consider the situation. What part of your actions do you regret? How would you act differently if given a second chance? Would it make sense for you to communicate with the person who was affected by your behavior?

In some instances, offering a clear apology can support you in reaching a place of energetic closure, even if the other person involved doesn't accept your attempt to make amends. In other situations, the simple act of recognizing that your behavior was not acceptable and committing to make a change can bring you to neutrality.

The objective in addressing situations involving your own actions is to arrive at a place of emotional neutrality, so that your energy is not required to keep past regrets alive.

Your Own Inaction

If you failed to follow through on something you now wish you would have, you may need to resolve your lack of action in order to avoid an insidious circle of thought, which I've coined "The Inaction Cycle." Inaction results in missed opportunities. Missed opportunities fuel fantasies about what could have been. Focusing on what could have been causes you to live in the neverland of "what if," instead of the reality of "what is." Living in fantasies of "what if" guarantees that you will never take the actions necessary to have a fabulous "what is." I've worked with countless people living in this cycle of fantasy and projection. Not only is this energetically expensive, it's a certain recipe for dissatisfaction with life.

Examples of inaction include failing to complete your degree, not following up on an interesting professional opportunity, failing to pursue a relationship with someone you were interested in, or putting off your study of a much-loved activity.

The important thing to identify specific to inaction is the reason you have regret. What do you think you would have gained had you acted on the opportunity you're remembering? What do you fear you missed out on? You cannot change the past, but you can create a compelling future. Get clear about the essence of what you wish you would have created or accomplished.

Once you've connected with your true intention, brainstorm several ways you could pursue that outcome today. It's been said that the longest journey begins with a single step. Your willingness to honestly assess what you regret, and embrace the possibility that you can create the essence of what you believe you missed out on can be a great source of drive and dynamic power.

Your Failure to Speak Your Truth

When you fail to let someone know what your true feelings are, or you allow another person to speak to you in a way you find unacceptable, you undermine your self-respect. This is energetically depleting, not to mention personally demoralizing.

Many times, women have difficulty letting someone know when they're angry or hurt. That's generally because we aren't comfortable with confrontation. We haven't been taught to communicate with clarity and constructive feedback, so we repress our emotions.

When you consistently censor yourself, eventually one of three things will happen—you will numb out emotionally, you will make yourself physically sick, or you will explode at the most inopportune moment. (We have all had those explosive moments. While it may feel great to rage like a banshee, I'm here to tell you there is a better way.)

Please understand that when you don't speak up for yourself you begin to compile an inventory of experiences that cause you to feel frustrated, sad, despondent, or completely furious. It takes a great deal of energy to fuel these emotions! Examples of such situations include allowing your mate to use an unacceptable tone of voice with you or allowing others to tease or criticize you.

If you find yourself in this type of situation frequently, it will be important for you to get comfortable with confrontation. Your willingness to be momentarily uncomfortable and to communicate with assertive clarity will support you in increasing both your energy and your self-respect. I use a five-part formula when helping my clients learn to speak up for themselves.

• *Step One* – Clearly describe the problem, as you see it, to the person involved.

• *Step Two* – Specifically let the other party know what part of his or her behavior was unacceptable to you.

• *Step Three* – Let the other person know how the situation made you feel.

• *Step Four* – Ask the other person for the specific solution you seek. This may require that you ask the person to change his or her behavior in some way. If this is the case, be very clear about the behavioral change you require. If you want an apology, ask for it.

• *Step Five* – This other person has free will and may see the situation much differently than you do. It's possible that he or she will not be willing to comply with your wishes. You must be ready and willing to let the other person know what you plan to do if he or she won't comply with your request. This may mean that you let the other know you can't have a relationship with him or her any longer, or that you'll have to limit the time you spend with him or her. Understand what your alternatives are and be willing to follow them through.

The core issue in learning to communicate on your own behalf goes far beyond the management of your energy. Truly, this skill will allow you to build your reserves of self-confidence and self-respect. The increase you'll experience in your level of vitality is simply an added bonus.

Someone Else's Unacceptable Actions

Human beings thrive on interaction. The most beautiful experiences we'll have in our lives will likely involve our connection with others. Unfortunately, some of the most difficult or traumatic experiences in our lives become part of our experience as a result of our interaction with other people.

If you have been physically, sexually, or emotionally abused, you have been on the worst possible receiving end of this human reality. If you've been the victim of abuse, it is quite possible that you will need the help of a good therapist to reach a place of closure. This program is not designed to address your experience under these circumstances. If you are in this position, I urge you to seek the help of a qualified, licensed mental health professional to achieve resolution.

This program is designed to help you move through any number of perceived slights that fall outside of outright abuse. An unacceptable behavior is an improper or inappropriate action, directed at you by another person, that causes you to have a negative emotional response. Examples of an unacceptable behavior include a family member snubbing you at an event, a co-worker spreading a rumor about you at the office, or a friend repeatedly standing you up when you commit to seeing each other.

The easiest way to determine whether or not you have any work to do in this area is to take an inventory of the people and events in your life. If there are individuals or experiences in your life that cause you to have a strong emotional reaction, it's highly probable you have unfinished business with them.

Take inventory of the people in your life and the experiences that stand out for you. If you discover that you have unresolved emotions around a person or event, move through the six-step model below to support you in reaching closure.

• *Step One* – Describe the event or experience. What happened, and why isn't this okay?

• *Step Two* – Connect with your emotions. How did this experience make you feel?

• *Step Three* – Identify what needs to happen for you to feel finished with your experience. Do you need to have a conversation with the person? Do you want an apology? Do you simply need to connect with your own emotions?

• *Step Four* – Get clear about your resolution path. If the situation involves another person, do you want him or her in your life or would you like to end the relationship? Do you feel a need to talk with the person about the incident, or would you prefer to put your feelings down on paper?

• *Step Five* – Allow yourself to fully feel the emotions that exist at the core of this issue. Let yourself be angry. Let yourself be sad. Many times, an emotion needs to be fully felt before you can let it go. Give yourself permission to experience and release your emotions.

• *Step Six* – Take action. Write the letter. Have the meeting. Do whatever you feel you need to do to reach closure.

In many instances, a repetitively inappropriate person may need to be removed from your life. In other instances, the person you've communicated with may work to change his or her behavior. The outcome of your acknowledgement and communication is much less important than your willingness to reclaim your emotional reserves.

Wrapping It Up

The energy you have invested in keeping regrets or conflicts alive will serve you in a far greater capacity when channeled toward more productive thoughts and activities. Your willingness to speak up for yourself, to forgive yourself for mistakes you've made, and to require people to treat you with respect will restore your emotional vitality. Then, you can focus your power on creating the results you want in your life.

CALL TO ACTION – INCREASE YOUR EMOTIONAL ENERGY

This activity is designed to liberate your energy from experiences you may have stored in your emotional inventory. These situations can be more difficult to understand and resolve, but they pack an incredible energetic punch once they're released. It is especially important to remember that you don't need to address every situation in your inventory to benefit from work in this area.

- Identify one situation in your emotional inventory that you feel ready to address. Get clear about what you require to resolve the situation.
  - Do you simply need to process it? If so, writing a letter allowing yourself to express your feelings may be enough to reach resolution.
  - Would you like an apology or a changed behavior from the other person? If so, on paper, work through the process I've outlined for you. Once you're clear about what you'd like to communicate, arrange to have a conversation with the other person during a time when you will be uninterrupted.
  - Do you need to make amends or take action on your own behalf? If so, get clear about what you're sorry for, or the circumstances you'd like to create for yourself. Use the strategies in this section to support you in addressing your oversight.
- Decide to work through only one item at a time and allow yourself to move at a comfortable pace. Seek the support of a close friend, family member, or your coach, and remember that small steps will lead you to the energetic liberation you seek.

Remember the tortoise and the hare: Slow and steady wins the race. Take small steps each day, and you will restore your emotional energy reserves.

KEY LEARNING POINTS

- You require energy to support every thought, word, action, and interaction in your life, and you have a limited amount of it available to you each day.
- Your energy is impacted by physical, mental, and emotional factors. Your commitment to proactively manage these factors will support you in creating the life you desire.

• Your physical energy is affected by the way you manage your environment and the way you care for your body. Committing to take great care of your physical world will infuse you with power and vitality.

• Your mental energy is influenced by the inventory of to-dos and projects you store in your memory bank. Proactively structuring your responsibilities will free your mental power.

• The emotional factor of energy has a powerful effect on your vitality and your sense of self. Treating other people with respect, taking action on your own behalf, and communicating clearly will help you maximize your emotional power.

ALIGN YOUR FOCUS:
THE PRIORITY COMPASS

Now that you've started to reclaim your energy, it's time to decide how you're going to use it. In this chapter, I'd like to challenge you to stop managing your time. Instead, I'd like you to consider managing your priorities.

Time is similar to energy in that it is finite. You get only 24 hours a day, 7 days a week, 365 days a year. Once you've used a moment, it is gone forever. The process of using your time effectively becomes possible when you begin to view it as a commodity that you have the choice to spend—or invest.

When you invest, you essentially allocate your resources to something you believe will give you a positive return. Most people understand the use of investments as they relate to money. You commit your capital to the financial instruments you believe will net an increase in your principal or a payment of interest. You also invest your financial resources in the activities or possessions you think will give you security, satisfaction, or pleasure.

Do you view your time with as much consideration as you view your money? It's likely you were schooled to value your financial resources and to use them in ways that support your family, your goals, and your life. It's also probable that you were never taught to consider your time so carefully.

I would bet that you would not burn a dollar bill. Yet, you may be willing to burn through an hour of your time based on someone else's demands. This is a direct result of the way you've been conditioned to view time—as expendable or renewable. Once your perspective shifts and you begin to view time as a valuable commodity, you will begin to make commitments more carefully, which will allow you to create a rich and balanced life experience.

THE RESOURCE OF TIME

Establishing a sense of equilibrium in your life not only requires that you acknowledge the limited nature of time, it also mandates that you be incredibly selective about how you allocate this precious resource.

If you have not proactively decided how you'd like to use your time, it's possible that a good deal of your day is committed to other people's demands, to items that seem urgent, or in response to what you believe is expected of you. If you've taken this approach to managing your calendar, I would guess you have very little time left over to invest in what matters to you.

At the end of each week, do you feel exhausted, frustrated, and burnt-out? Do you sometimes wonder why you can't seem to get control and question what is wrong with you? If this sounds familiar, I'm here to assure you that there is nothing wrong with you. You simply need a structure to support you in using your moments more proactively.

This structure will include connecting with your priorities, managing your calendar according to what matters, and establishing powerful habits.

CONNECTING WITH YOUR PRIORITIES

A priority is something that is important to you, or something that needs your attention in the present. Your personal priorities define how you invest time within your life. Your professional priorities guide your allocation of the time committed to your work.

Making the decision to invest your time according to your priorities not only supports the effective use of each moment, it also paves the road to a high-quality life. It creates a structure for you to make decisions that help you experience life on your terms and gives you permission to turn away from requirements that don't support your aspirations.

Your life experience is defined by your personal priorities. Areas factoring into your personal list could include your health, your relationships, your career, your financial well-being, your spirituality, your home environment, your personal growth and development, and your ability to participate in your community.

Your professional experience is equally affected by your use of priorities in making commitments at work. Invariably, you manage a multitude of demands on the job. Your ability to identify the most important areas to invest your time and energy in will allow you to operate more effectively and enjoyably each day.

Items that could weigh in on your professional priority list include maintaining inter-office or industry relationships, identifying new prospects or opportunities, managing existing client relationships, developing products or solutions, attending important meetings, increasing your industry or product knowledge, and managing communications.

Most of the things on your lists will reflect your personal desires and interests. Other areas will need to be included because they require your attention in order for your life and work to function smoothly. For example, running errands, paying bills, and responding to email may not feel like satisfying activities but they must be completed to support your lifestyle.

CALL TO ACTION – DEFINE YOUR PRIORITIES

Set aside twenty to thirty minutes to move through this activity. Try to arrange for an uninterrupted period of time, which allows you to consider the areas of your life and work that are truly important to you. Create a list that reflects who you are, not a list that reflects what you think other people expect of you.

To support your thought process, I've provided you with an example of a list one of my clients created.

DINA'S LIST

Personal Priorities

- Spending quality time with my husband
- Spending quality time with my kids
- Taking care of my body—working out and eating well
- Taking time out for fun and recreation
- Managing the family finances
- Running the household—cleaning, errands, coordinating family schedule
- Spending time with friends

Professional Priorities

- Leading and mentoring my employees
- Managing existing client relationships
- Developing new business
- Maintaining relationships in my industry
- Managing the company's finances
- Contributing to industry panel discussions
- Continuing to learn and grow my skill base

Now it's your turn.

MY PERSONAL PRIORITIES

1. _____
2. _____
3. _____
4. _____
5. _____

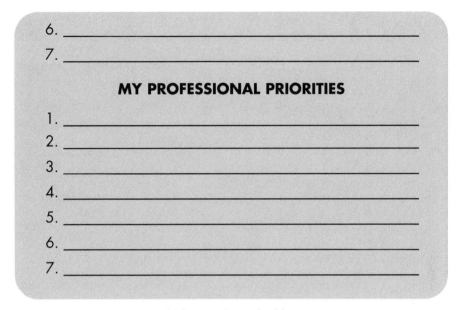

6. _____

7. _____

MY PROFESSIONAL PRIORITIES

1. _____

2. _____

3. _____

4. _____

5. _____

6. _____

7. _____

Wrapping It Up

When you make the choice to honestly define what matters to you, the possibility for life and work balance is created. It's quite likely that your schedule will remain full, even after moving through this exercise. The difference is that you will be busy with things that matter to you. You'll be living your priorities. As a result, you'll have the opportunity to experience a much greater level of joy, satisfaction, and happiness each day. Ultimately, that's what we're all looking for.

MANAGE YOUR CALENDAR ACCORDING TO WHAT MATTERS

The potential to experience joy, satisfaction, and happiness lives in your calendar. You will begin to experience more of what matters to you when you schedule less of what doesn't.

Now that you've identified the priorities you'd like to invest in, it's important to evaluate how you're currently spending your time. If your calendar does not reflect the priorities you've defined for yourself, it will be necessary for you to make some changes in order to create room in your schedule.

CALL TO ACTION – COMPLETE A TIME EVALUATION

• I'd like you to open your calendar and look at the commitments you've made for the next two weeks.

• How many of your commitments support the priorities you just established? How many do not?

At this point in the process, many people find themselves a bit dumbfounded. It is not uncommon to identify that more than half of the activities you've committed to your schedule do not support your highest priorities.

If you're spending more than half of your time catering to the demands of others, doing things because you think you should do them, or making commitments because you aren't comfortable declining, it's quite likely you're unbalanced, overwhelmed, resentful, and unfulfilled at the end of most days.

It's time to change that! You can support the people in your life, fulfill your responsibilities, make time for things that are important to you, and create a sense of balance in your life.

CLIENT STORY – ISABELLE

Isabelle was a polished, articulate, focused young professional. She was a happily married mother in her early thirties who had made quite a name for herself in real estate. She was also in the midst a self-described time management crisis.

She shared with me that she felt overwhelmed with the number of responsibilities she was juggling in her life and work. She let me know that she didn't feel she was making progress on the important projects in either area. Rather, she was burdened, even angered, by the many social and volunteer responsibilities associated with her daughter's school and a professional organization she belonged to. She couldn't remember the last time she'd been out to dinner with her girlfriends, and she was ready to make a change.

I asked her to track her activities for one week and bring her findings back to our next meeting. During our next session, we moved through the exercise of designing her personal and professional priorities. We then compared the priorities she'd defined with the week she'd just experienced. She was astounded. Only two of the priorities on her professional list and one from her personal list had made it into her schedule, yet she'd been busy from early morning until late into the evening every day of the week. No wonder she was burnt-out. She was killing herself to accomplish someone else's priorities!

We made a list of all of her current commitments and evaluated how they either supported or detracted from her ability to live within her priority framework. Not surprisingly, over half of her commitments just didn't fit. I told Isabelle that if she wanted to make room for what mattered, she had to get rid of what didn't.

She took a deep breath and shared the trepidation she felt at the prospect of withdrawing from the social and volunteer activities that weren't supporting her. We prepared a script she could follow when having each of the conversations she would need to engage in if she wanted to free herself. She decided the momentary discomfort was worth the possibilities her newly freed-up calendar would hold.

Over the next four weeks, Isabelle resigned from two committees at her daughter's school, committing to lend her time in the classroom one afternoon a month. She withdrew from all but one committee in the professional organization she belonged to, and she completely withdrew from the non-profit organization she'd volunteered for.

In her newfound time, she began to incorporate the activities that she'd noted on her priority list. She was able to begin riding her bike again, an activity she loved. She started seeing her girlfriends a couple of times each month and began to enjoy a date night each week with her husband. Best of all, she began working on a special project with her daughter, an activity that simply wasn't possible in her previously overwhelming schedule.

Three months after concluding our work together, not only was Isabelle enjoying her full yet fulfilling schedule, her business had increased by thirty percent. She couldn't believe that the simple changes we'd made had changed her life, yet they had.

Isabelle had the foresight to cry uncle. She knew she was at the end of her rope, and she sought help. She was willing to make some hard decisions and engage in some difficult conversations. As a result, she is enjoying her husband, her daughter, her friends, her work, and her life more fully.

The Rules of Time Management

You will succeed or fail in this endeavor based on your willingness to consistently invest your time in support of the priorities you've established. This becomes possible when you remove requests and commitments that fall outside of your priority structure. In short, this means you're going to have to get very good at saying the dreaded "n" word—*no*.

Many of my clients have had a difficult time saying *no*—due to their desire to avoid disappointing others and their aversion to feeling uncomfortable. To preserve your time for things that matter to you, you must be willing to experience temporary discomfort. This requires dedication to the focused management of your schedule and calls for you to develop the courage to risk upsetting or disappointing others. The following rules may help you in flexing your "no" muscle.

Be Authentic

Your priority list must reflect what you authentically hold in esteem versus what you believe should be important to you. Creating a list based on what you believe is expected of you, or out of fear about what others might think of you, is a recipe for stress and failure.

Be honest when creating your priority blueprint. It can serve you, acting as a compass to support you in making decisions about where to invest your time and energy. If you don't define your list based on your truth, you will be living someone else's. I know you don't want that reality or you wouldn't be reading this book.

Remember that you don't need to share your priorities with the people in your life or even let anyone know that you're using them. If you're unsure about what others might think, I encourage you to keep your list private and allow it to be a quiet resource you rely on to make good choices. Whether or not you share your strategy, please allow your list to be your own.

Place Yourself on Your List

You are going to notice a theme clearly woven throughout the fabric of this program—the theme of self-care. When you commit to taking care of yourself, you become more powerfully able to take care of everyone else in your life. While you may feel an initial resistance to placing yourself on your own list, believing it would be selfish to do so, I strongly encourage you to invest in taking care of you. As we move through each step in our process, I'll remind you of this core principal and make suggestions about how to do so.

For now, I'd like to stress that in instances when you refuse to address your physical, mental, emotional, and spiritual needs, your personal growth stalls. You run out of energy, get frustrated more easily, and lose your sense of well-being. Conversely, when you begin to nurture yourself and address your own needs, your spirit soars. You begin to handle the details of life and work with a greater level of ease, you feel an enhanced sense of appreciation, and your personal sense of happiness grows.

You don't need to forego meeting your responsibilities or caring for the people in your life to carve out time to care for yourself. You simply need to decide that it's important to give yourself a bit of nurturing.

When you do, you will be able to give more to every area of your life. For the rest of this program, I challenge you to take care of yourself *at least as well* as you take care of everyone else!

Know Your Own Worth

If you don't believe you're worthy of acceptance and friendship, you will try to earn your way into both. The fear of unworthiness is at the root of many unproductive behaviors, such as accepting invitations you aren't interested in, agreeing to requests that don't compliment your priorities, and taking on responsibilities that detract from your own well-being. The disease to please may not kill you, but it will significantly detract from the quality of your life.

You do not need to earn your way into love, acceptance, or friendship. You are worthy of all those things, simply because you exist. If you're not sure you believe that—and many women aren't—I encourage you to begin building your confidence muscles.

Take time out each day to recognize your strengths, congratulate yourself for your accomplishments, and acknowledge the contribution you make to the lives of others. Decide to use your time and energy in support of your life and work priorities and take action from a place of strength and commitment to yourself.

As you begin to make decisions that support your priorities, you will create momentum in your life. You will begin to experience the results of your discipline, and this will increase your self-confidence. Your sense of worth and value will deepen with every decision and every acknowledgement.

Don't worry if this approach feels unnatural at first. I've seen many clients become more confident as a result of acting their way into confidence. Soon, your esteem will increase and you will naturally approach your life with a greater level of confidence and a deeper level of respect for yourself.

Say Goodbye to Takers

If you've been living as a pleaser, there are undoubtedly takers around you. A taker is a person who uses your time, energy, money, and resources without giving anything back in return. I liken these individuals to parasites, and they will begin to disappear when you start saying *no.*

While it's difficult to lose a friend, the reality is that these people were not your friends to begin with. They were opportunists and were participating in your life at your expense. You will succeed far more rapidly without them taking advantage of you.

Make a commitment to stand your ground and invest yourself in only those requests that meet your priorities or interest you. Prepare yourself in advance to decline invitations or requests that don't. Anticipate the inevitable shedding of the takers in your life and celebrate the opening you're creating for a higher quality of person to enter in their place.

Evaluating Opportunities

Ideally, your priorities will help you make decisions about what to commit your time to. When considering a new opportunity, evaluate whether or not the invitation sounds interesting to you. If it doesn't, reserve the right to say *no!*

If an invitation seems interesting, consider whether or not the commitment supports your priorities. If it doesn't, minimally evaluate whether or not it might detract from them. If it does not meet your priorities and has the potential to detract from your ability to invest your time in what matters to you, say *no*.

If you feel that the opportunity fits within your priorities, and it's interesting, consider committing yourself. Make sure to understand why you find the opportunity exciting, and clarify any expectations the inviting party will have of you once you throw your hat into the ring.

Pledge yourself from a clear and positive place. If you feel any misgivings about consigning yourself, stop! From this point on, decide that you will only make commitments that compliment your priorities and feel good to you.

Reserve the Right to Think About It

It is quite probable that you are conditioned to immediately agree to any type of invitation you receive. A great way to break this pattern is to decide you will not commit to anything on the spot.

Instead, when you receive a request or invitation, let the requestor know that you'll need to check your schedule and get back to him or her. This allows you to thoughtfully evaluate the situation and provides you with a buffer in the event that you decide to decline. It's much easier to forgo a request on the telephone or via email than it is to do so in person. Old habits die hard. Give yourself some wiggle room when conditioning your new scheduling habits.

Do Away with Elaborate Excuses

I was watching Oprah Winfrey one afternoon when she said something that changed how I say *no*. She said, "*No* is a complete sentence."

I'd never thought about it that way. I'd always believed that I had to provide an excuse if I wasn't able to do something I'd been asked to do. It took a message from my television to wake me up to my right to say *no*.

The next time someone asks you to take on a project or attend an event that doesn't support your priorities, simply respond with "No, I can't do that, but thank you for thinking of me." Breathe deeply to quiet your thundering heart and move on to another topic of conversation.

CALL TO ACTION – TARGET TIME WASTERS

• **Identify at least five commitments or scheduled activities that are wasting your valuable time.** Examples could include volunteering for an organization you no longer enjoy, running errands for others, attending social events with people you don't care for, participating in water cooler gossip, or failing to commit your day to activities that are important to you.

• **Name your alternative.** Could one of your priority areas move into the timeslot that one of your time wasters currently occupies? List the five commitments you would prefer to make in place of your current time wasters.

• **Conclude your commitment to non-priority activities.** If the item is a one-time engagement, contact the host or requestor and let him or her know you have a conflict. If your commitment is ongoing in nature, let your contact person know you cannot participate any longer.

• **Schedule something from your priority list into the open time that appears as a result of allowing yourself to say *no*.**

Wrapping It Up

The first few times you remove a commitment from your life or decline a request, you may be wildly uncomfortable. It is at these times that you must stay centered in the knowledge that you are choosing yourself.

Every time you make a decision to say *yes* to one thing, you are saying *no* to multiple others simultaneously. You may not be aware of this, but it is fact. Until you are able to say *no* to the demands and requests of others, you will never be able to say *yes* to you.

Ultimately, it is better to disappoint the requestor whom you will not remember forty years from now, than to look back at your life and realize that the person you disappointed was yourself.

ESTABLISH POWERFUL HABITS

The quality of your daily experience is directly impacted by your habits. A habit is a conditioned pattern of behavior. In many instances, habits become conditioned to the point of automation. Under these circumstances, it's not uncommon for you to engage in habituated behavior without even thinking about what you're doing. You undoubtedly have many common habits, such as drinking coffee with the morning paper, walking the dog, or unwinding with the television at night.

Habits can be empowering and can serve you in creating circumstances that help you build the kind of life you want to live. They can also be disempowering, causing you to veer off course from your ideal.

In Step 6, we'll take a close look at your habits, and I'll challenge you to differentiate between those that serve you and those that don't. In this step, we're going to get started with some basic information about the two kinds of habits—habits of thought and habits of action—and I'm going to provide you with examples of the habits most commonly used by balanced, fulfilled, successful people.

Habits of Thought

Your habitual thoughts shape your attitude and govern how you perceive the world around you. Ultimately, the interpretation of every experience you have is shaped by your habitual thoughts. Do you expect things to go well or when something good happens do you find yourself waiting for the other shoe to drop? Do you see opportunity when entering new situations or do you focus on obstacles?

Identifying and shifting habitual thoughts that don't serve you will significantly improve your life. When ending an old pattern of thinking, your chance of success will increase exponentially when you *replace* your old idea with a new one that does serve you. In this way, rather than using willpower to stop yourself from thinking in a habituated way, you begin to condition a new habit of thought to take the place of the old. Because this strategy relies on conditioning instead of willpower, you will be much more successful with this approach.

I've provided you with a snapshot of some of my favorite thought patterns. You can use these habits to replace limiting thoughts, or you can simply begin integrating them into your life. Either way, they will serve you in any situation.

The Habit of Gratitude

How many people, things, and privileges do you take for granted each day? Have you established an attitude of appreciation? Gratitude is one of the most powerful emotions on the planet. When you develop a habit of noticing and acknowledging the abundance in your life, not only will you experience a greater sense of wellness and fulfillment, you will also expand your ability to deal with circumstances that aren't ideal.

So many people invest their energy in noticing what's not working, what's wrong, or what needs to be fixed. The simple shift of acknowledging how much is right with your world can change the way you look at every problem and every opportunity in front of you.

For the next twenty-one days, I challenge you to find five things to be grateful for at the end of every day. You could acknowledge the beauty of nature, the softness of your pet's fur, the love you feel from a family member, or the warm food on your table at night.

Take a moment every day to be consciously thankful for all you have. As you condition this habit of thought, you'll feel an increased sense of joy and happiness and you'll create even more to be grateful for.

The Habit of Possibility

Are you an optimist or a pessimist? When faced with a problem, do you see catastrophe or opportunity? Study after study has proven that optimistic people lead happier, and in some instances, longer lives than their pessimistic counterparts.

Noticing the downside of a situation can be very productive. It's not possible to correct a problem if you refuse to acknowledge it's there. The danger in this thought pattern is in the lack of hope most pessimists feel. Their shortage of belief causes them to question their ability to create the results they want in life, so they are less likely to work toward their goals than optimists are.

When you believe in possibility, you invest yourself in the notion that the circumstances you'd like to create are achievable. This makes you much more likely to take action and create the results you want in any situation. This mindset does not suggest that you don't recognize problems or acknowledge circumstances that fall short of your standards. It simply invites you to invest yourself in the belief that you can change whatever it is that currently falls short of your expectations.

Next time you're presented with a problem or you have the opportunity to work on an important project, invest yourself in possibility. Look for ways to make your situation work, search out resources, and own the personal actions you can take to contribute to the situation. Invest your energy in the habit of possibility and you'll be amazed at the results you create in your life.

The Habit of Acceptance

You will face problems and disappointments in your life. Things will not always turn out the way you'd like them to. Your feelings might be hurt. People may not live up to your expectations. You could lose a job or be required to deal with a health problem.

When facing a disappointing situation, you have two choices: You can accept your current circumstances and commit yourself to correcting them or you can wallow in anger and regret over the hand you've been dealt.

More energy is wasted resisting circumstances than in almost any other area of life. When you resist an event, you direct your time, emotions, and resources toward fighting inevitability. This approach results in angry, hopeless, victimized emotions and ultimately leads to either frustrated inaction or wasted motion.

I'm not suggesting that you lie down and accept a dissatisfying situation or unacceptable circumstances. I am challenging you to get real, acknowledge the truth about every situation you find yourself in, and decide you're going to invest your energy in making things the way you want them to be versus railing against reality.

Acceptance is an incredibly effective pattern of thought. When you condition this habit, you increase your ability to handle any circumstance in life.

Habits of Action

Your habitual actions create your reality. This concept is best illustrated with the widely accepted notion of cause and effect. Every action you take (or fail to take) creates a corresponding result. If you're unhappy with the results in your life, the most effective way to change them is to adjust the action you're taking.

As with habits of thought, the most effective way to stop taking an action that isn't serving you is to replace it with a new and more empowering one. Shifting your habits of action to the proactive strategies I've outlined below will help you create momentum and establish a greater sense of equilibrium.

The Habit of Self-Care

Remember a few pages back when I introduced you to our self-care theme? Well, here we are again. How do you take care of yourself? Do you make time for exercise? Do you eat healthful foods? Do you feed your mind with new information or your spirit with the company of people who love you?

The habits you establish in support of taking care of yourself physically, mentally, emotionally, and spiritually quite literally form the underpinning of your quality of life. If you habitually overeat, smoke cigarettes, or drink alcohol to excess, it's likely your patterns are damaging your health. If you regularly choose to spend the evening with your television set instead of your best friend, you may be robbing yourself of much needed friendship and connection. If you insist on putting everyone else's needs ahead of your own, you're creating your own empty, angry martyrdom.

If you make no other change as a result of reading this book, commit to improving your self-care habits—and your life will change. Everything in your world is a direct reflection of you. When you do not take care of yourself, it's not possible for you to fully take care of anyone or anything else. This robs you of the opportunity to live fully into your potential.

For the next twenty-one days, commit to developing one new empowering habit of self-care. You could begin exercising, commit to eating more fruits and vegetables, schedule a weekly lunch with a friend, or commit to a daily time-out for yourself. Develop the habit of nurturing your body, mind, heart, and spirit and your whole world will blossom.

The Habit of Self-Connection

It's difficult to create the life of your dreams when you've lost touch with what your dreams are. Our busy society makes it very easy for you to focus on the external demands of life and disconnect from your internal world.

There is a magical, all-knowing, intuitive force inside of you. This powerful authenticity rests quietly in your heart, just waiting to be tapped. When you give yourself a few quiet moments each day to re-establish this connection—through journaling, meditation, or quiet contemplation—you become more serene, more centered, and more certain about what you want. Your willingness to spend ten quiet minutes with yourself each day can change your world.

Schedule a time each day to get reacquainted with yourself. This could be in the morning before getting started with your day or in the evening as you unwind to go to bed. Ten short minutes, observed daily, will provide you with the opportunity to reconnect with the woman you are and might introduce you to the real power of the woman you are meant to be.

The Habit of Play

How long has it been since you had a completely unscheduled day? Can you remember the last time you did something for the sheer fun of doing it? Do you remember what *fun* is?

You probably have many memories of your childhood playtime. This unscheduled, creative, joyous time allowed you to connect with others, enjoy yourself, and use your creativity. You might have loved being active—playing tag or riding your bike—or you could have preferred playing with dolls or acting out make-believe games. Think back to the young girl you were. What did you love about coming out to play? How long has it been since that little girl had some fun?

As an adult woman, it's highly probable that your drive to be responsible, coupled with a life on hyper-drive has extinguished the play in your life. Now is the time to bring it back! What would you like to play? Does a special outing come to mind, or do you think it might be fun to resume a hobby you used to love? Either way, it's imperative you make some small amount of time to bring fun back into your life.

It doesn't matter if you do this once a week or once a month. The point is to begin conditioning the habit of lightness, being in the moment, and embracing the joy of life. When you do, you'll find that even the most mundane tasks start to feel more satisfying.

CALL TO ACTION – SHIFT YOUR HABITS

To identify your habits and evaluate where you might want to shift your behavior, answer the following questions for both your habits of thought and your habits of action.

- What habits hold you back or decrease the quality of your life?
- What do you say to yourself when you indulge these patterns?
- What kind of situations trigger them?
- What habits would serve you better?

On a sheet of paper or an index card, draw a line down the center. Write each of your old habits on the left side of the page or card. On the right side, write the new habit you want to shift to, next to the old habit you want it to replace.

Select one habit to start with. For the next four weeks, catch yourself each time you begin to move into your old pattern and immediately replace it with the new one. A new habit can be conditioned in as little as twenty-one days. Make your commitment, and vigilantly hold yourself to it. Not only will you experience a surge of confidence as a result of your dedication, you'll also begin to enjoy happier days.

Wrapping It Up

The quality of your life increases when your habits improve. Be willing to take a good look at your patterns. We all have habits that need to shift. Don't beat yourself up about where you are. Instead, look forward. Start small and make your changes one habit at a time. Our greatest journeys begin with one single step, and the most amazing lives are built one habit at a time.

KEY LEARNING POINTS

• It becomes possible to use your time effectively when you begin to view it as a finite commodity that you have the choice to spend—or invest.

• Establishing a list of priorities for your life and work, and making commitments based on that list, allows the things that are important to you to exist in your life.

• In order to say *yes* to yourself, you must be willing to say *no* to others.

• Your habits shape your life. To improve the quality of your life, improve the quality of your habits.

• It is easier to change a poor habit when you replace it with a more empowering alternative. Shifting your behavior to your new pattern allows you to condition your new habit, instead of resisting your old one.

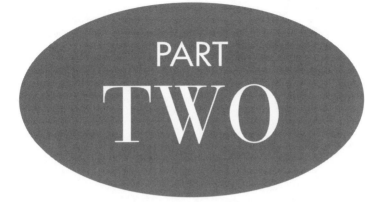

PART

TWO

ESTABLISH YOUR
FOUNDATION

DEFINE WHAT DRIVES YOU:
THE POWER OF NEEDS AND BELIEFS

Kathy's pulse was racing. She could feel beads of sweat forming on her upper lip, and her heart was pumping so wildly she thought it might beat right out of her chest. Her fists were clenched, and her blood was boiling. She looked at the clock again.

She knew she was overreacting. Her husband was only fifteen minutes late. But he was *always* late! She felt unappreciated and uncared for. She was angry, and she'd had enough. She didn't want to fight with her husband tonight. It was their anniversary, but she couldn't think rationally. All she could focus on was how hurt and unseen she felt. When her husband opened the door, she let him have it!

Have you ever had a similar experience? Honestly, how many times have you found yourself indulging that sort of out-of-body sensation that accompanies throwing a full-fledged fit? At times like these, you know that your behavior is not constructive. In fact, you may be entirely out-of-line. Yet, you don't stop. You *can't* stop. You *don't want* to stop! In these moments, you have literally been hijacked by your basic human needs. Momentarily, at least, you've lost control.

It's time to take your control back! I've seen one too many women stop themselves from truly succeeding as a result of poorly met needs and limiting beliefs. These twin factors—needs and beliefs—literally shape the way you perceive and respond to your world. They drive your behavior—and if you're not conscious of them, they can drive you right into a ditch of dissatisfaction and despair.

In this step, we're going to put you back in the driver's seat. We're going to talk about your needs and the strategies you've developed to satisfy them, and we're going to take a look at your beliefs to make sure that your convictions are empowering you.

NEEDS

In working with clients, I've encountered a great deal of resistance surrounding needs. For some reason, we live in a society that perceives people who have needs as weak and unsavory. Yet the presence of needs does not make you weak. In fact, needs are universal and essential requirements that must be satisfied in order for you to live happily. They have been studied and documented for thousands of years, and *everyone* has them.

Needs in and of themselves are not good or bad. In fact, they're neutral. The strategies you've adopted to meet your needs, on the other hand, can be either empowering or disempowering. While you may not have control over the fact that your needs exist, you do have absolute governance over the strategies you put in place to meet them.

Whether or not you are aware of them, you currently have and use a set of strategies to meet each of your needs. Most of these strategies were developed unconsciously in the early part of your life and served as coping mechanisms that helped you meet your emotional and physical requirements. Essentially, as a young child, you learned what kind of behavior helped you get what you wanted. When a specific approach worked, you adapted, and began to use that method again and again. If a certain approach didn't work, you tested new methods until you found the ones that supported you.

In a nutshell, human beings do what works. If one of your needs in early childhood was to get attention, which is a common and universal requirement, and you learned that whenever you behaved badly you would get attention—even negative attention—chances are you developed a pattern of bad behavior.

While your strategy may not have served a higher need or supported you in being your best self, it worked. Your brain, being the efficient machine that it is, then catalogued this information. Now, as a responsible, thinking, upstanding adult, you may be surprised to find yourself engaging in fits of bad behavior whenever you feel lacking in attention. Yet, you will continue to engage in this kind of behavior until you consciously develop a more empowering alternative.

CLIENT PROFILE – JENNIFER

I began working with Jennifer to increase her personal effectiveness. She was having difficulty working with a number of her colleagues, and she'd received a poor performance review as a result of her challenges relating.

Within the first few moments of our initial meeting, it became apparent that Jennifer's needs were controlling her behavior. We discussed the concept of needs, and I asked her to keep a log of her interactions with co-workers in the coming week. I challenged her to assess how effective she thought each interaction was and to note her feelings at the end of each meeting. I also asked her to pay special attention to those times when she recognized that her behavior was not as constructive as it could be, making notes about her feelings specific to each of those occurrences.

When Jennifer and I met again, we reviewed her log. We noticed that she frequently lost her temper when her co-workers challenged her statements. We also noticed that if the attention of the group was directed at one of her peers instead of her, her outbursts would become more pronounced.

Upon further discussion, it became clear that Jennifer linked having the right answer to being accepted. She'd also made a connection between being the center of attention and her personal worth. In instances where Jennifer felt someone was telling her she didn't have the right answer, her fear of losing peer acceptance prompted her to act in an aggressive and defensive manner. When feeling a lack of attention, her uncertainty about her own worth caused her to turn her behavior up a notch in order to direct the attention of the group back to her.

While the emotional intent behind this unconscious response was positive—she was attempting to get her needs met with the strategies she'd learned would work—she was undermining the very results she wanted to create. Her abrupt manner had created a separation rather than an inclusive acceptance between her and her co-workers, and her attempts to manipulate group attention had caused others to avoid giving her the very thing she sought.

Jennifer and I embraced the needs that were driving her behavior and went to work on improving her strategies. We identified the triggers within her workday that caused her to react in unproductive ways, and we created tactics she could use to interrupt those old reactions—replacing them with more proactive responses.

Within two short weeks, Jennifer's co-workers were taking notice of the changes she'd started to make. Within six weeks, Jennifer's supervisor called her into his office to find out what she had done to turn herself around. Not only did this shift in behavior improve Jennifer's daily work experience, it created new opportunities for her. She is now the manager of a small project management group and uses the skills she developed while we worked together to help her team members increase their own personal effectiveness.

If there is any area of your life where you find yourself stuck, moving in circles, dissatisfied, or solving the same problems over and over again, I guarantee that your needs are the source of your problem. In every instance where you've adopted poor strategies to meet your needs, you are literally standing in the way of your own success.

The good news is: Once you identify and proactively satisfy your needs, your capacity to embrace the fullness of life will astound you. You will take control of your behavior. Then, and only then, will you have the opportunity to experience the fulfillment you seek. It's time to step into your power. Are you ready to get out of your own way?

THE FIVE PRIMARY NEEDS

While the strategies you've adopted to meet your needs will be unique to you, your needs in and of themselves are quite universal. Literally, you share these requirements with every person you come into contact with. (This realization may allow you to be a bit more compassionate the next time you witness one of those irrational full-fledged fits we spoke about earlier in this step.)

The process of identifying and improving upon the strategies you use can transform your life. As you dive into this process, remember that your needs are not good or bad, but your strategies are absolutely empowering or disempowering. Our objective is to discover your unique approach and improve upon it when necessary.

The Need for Security

Your need for security is based on survival and is your most primal requirement. This category includes both the need to meet your physiological requirements and the desire to preserve your safety.

Physiological needs include food, shelter, water, elimination, and sleep. These are the inherent requirements of biological survival. You must nourish and hydrate yourself, you need housing, you must make time for sleep, and your body must remove waste from your system. In essence, you must address the needs of your body before you're able to address the needs of your emotion or intellect.

Related to your need to take care of your body is your need to protect it. While fundamentally rooted in your desire to protect your physical safety, this requirement also includes the need to preserve your emotional, intellectual, and material safety.

Have you ever been preoccupied with worry? Perhaps you were concerned about your job amidst a downsizing trend in the economy. Maybe you were worried that you would not have adequate financial resources to pay your bills. Perhaps someone close to you was diagnosed with a life-threatening illness.

At times like these, you were likely focused on your fears about the problems facing you. You probably weren't considering new opportunities or allowing yourself to envision your life purpose. On the contrary, you were biologically driven to address the potential threat to your security—to the exclusion of all else.

If your need for safety is not satisfied, whether the threat you perceive is real or imagined, you will live in dedication to creating the security you seek. Your energy will be invested in protecting yourself. You will not seek out new opportunity, you will not engage with activities you associate with risk, you will avoid change, and you will live in a defensive state. This is not the way to step into your potential, yet it's how many people live.

Did you know that your brain cannot distinguish between real and imagined threats? When you focus on what you fear might happen, your brain deals with the scenario you're worried about as if it is actually happening. Your body moves into fight-or-flight mode, a substance called cortisol is released in your system, and you have difficulty focusing on anything other than the perceived threat. As a result of your worry, your brain literally moves your body into survival mode when the thing you're worried about hasn't even happened yet!

Living in survival mode creates a host of difficulties, not the least of which is physical. The most productive way to move yourself beyond this limitation is to proactively meet your need for security.

The approach that works for you may be very different from the approach that works for your best friend. For this reason, you'll need to commit a short period of time to consider the tactics that will be most effective for you. To get you started, I've included several key strategies below.

• *Create Financial Security.* Tactics such as reserving a certain amount of money in the bank, using a plan to manage your financial life, owning your own home, or securing funds for retirement can be very effective in making you feel secure.

• *Maintain Good Health.* Meeting your physiological needs is a powerful way to support your security requirements. Productive behaviors in this area could include eating well, exercising, attending regular medical and dental appointments, or maintaining health insurance.

• *Establish Feelings of Control.* Having a plan for all aspects of your life can support your need to feel safe by providing you with a sense of clarity and direction. This strategy can be very productive in that it guides your focus and helps you manage your behavior. Keeping an orderly environment is another proactive way to meet your need for control. Having a place for everything you own gives you a sense of physical mastery, which greatly contributes to feelings of safety.

• *Instill Feelings of Protection.* Taking measures to ensure your physical safety will support your need to feel secure. Activities that could contribute to this strategy include installing a home alarm system or taking a self-defense class.

• *Establish Supportive Routines.* Maintaining a level of life predictability creates feelings of certainty. When you know what to expect, there is no need for you to prepare for the unknown. This kind of predictability is most effectively created by establishing supportive routines.

• *Embrace a Faith-Based Practice.* A sense of safety can also be created through the adoption of a spiritually based practice. Establishing a belief system in a power beyond you and making time to connect with that energy can ease your fears and anxieties, supporting you in feeling secure and protected.

Another way to identify safety strategies that will work for your unique circumstances is to think back to a time when you felt incredibly safe, and describe the conditions of that situation. Conversely, you can also think back to a time when you felt incredibly insecure, and identify the factors that played into that experience.

If you don't consciously decide how you're going to meet your need for safety, your unconscious patterns will do the job for you. More often than not, this will result in a life of limitation, fear, and worry. You deserve better than that!

Identify what you need to feel secure, evaluate the methods you currently use to meet your need, and consider how you might improve upon your current strategies.

The Need for Connection

Your need for connection manifests itself as a need to experience a sense of relatedness, to belong to a community, or to experience intimacy with another person. At its root, this drive dates back to our tribal ancestors. In tribal terms, your very survival depended upon your inclusion in the group. Tribal members ate, slept, and received protection as a result of being part of a unified structure. Rejection by the clan was equivalent to death.

At its most basic origins, your need for acceptance and the resulting fear of rejection is rooted in these ancestral social interaction models. While you don't need the tribe to provide food, shelter, or protection any longer, you do require community to satisfy your emotional requirements of inclusion, connection, and belonging.

The need for connection can manifest in a number of different ways. As you read through the examples that follow, consider which of these methods makes you feel most connected to others.

• *Include and Be Included.* Get involved in your family, organization, or community. Accept invitations to social functions. If you haven't received any invitations lately, extend some of your own. Let people know that you want to be involved with them. Your involvement with others will productively meet your need to be included as well as the needs of those you're involved with.

• *To Accept and Be Accepted.* Surrounding yourself with people who like and accept you *as you are* is imperative when meeting your need for connection. You can support this need by deciding you will act authentically with others, never pretending to be someone you aren't. If you find yourself in a situation where the real you is not being accepted, seek out a different situation! In keeping with this spirit, extend acceptance to others who are willing to be real with you. Not only does this tactic support your need for connection, it also supports your desire to be a good human being.

• *Love and Be Loved.* You need to both give and receive strong feelings of affection, approval, and affinity. You can create opportunities for this type of experience with significant others, family members, friends, children, and even animals. If hearing the words "I Love You" makes you feel loved, let the significant people in your life know that you need to hear those words! If being held creates feelings of loving connection, make sure that you create opportunities to hold and be held! The golden rules in meeting your need to feel connected through love are to ask for what you want and to give what you want to receive. When you adopt these two tactics, your connection needs will be thoroughly satisfied!

• *Create a Sense of Community.* Your willingness to establish a sense of social relatedness among your family, colleagues, neighborhood, and the organizations you belong to will increase your feelings of connectedness. Take an active interest in others and be willing to share details about yourself. Invest time in building relationships. Host the barbecue. Go out for cocktails after work. Attend the silent auction at school. Establishing a sense of community in your life and work is an incredibly productive way to satisfy your need for connection.

When your need for belonging and connection is satisfied, you will feel an incredible sense of well-being. What makes you feel connected? How are you currently meeting that need? Is there room for you to improve upon your current methods? Consider how you might enhance your current approach and enjoy an even greater sense of relatedness.

The Need to Be Autonomous

Your need for autonomy requires that you feel free to self-govern. When you have the power to act and speak freely, your sense of independence and spontaneity increases. Essentially, you must feel that your life is one of your choosing. You must believe that you have the ability to make decisions for yourself, to make your own plans, and to adjust your life direction should you decide to.

The need for autonomy can be satisfied in a number of highly productive ways. Invariably, small business owners have a strong need for autonomy. They address this desire by moving in an entrepreneurial direction and create a great deal of value in the process. Conversely, a less productive strategy for meeting this need could involve a resistance to commitment, which greatly hinders life and work progression.

Consider the following autonomy strategies. Which method most closely reflects the circumstances you require to meet this need?

• *Own the Truth of Choice.* This is an easily forgotten tenet. You are always free to choose. You *have* to do very little in your life. Granted, there may be repercussions associated with not taking certain actions, such as going to work or paying your bills, and it's a fact of life that things may happen to you that you have no control over. Still, you choose how you'll deal with whatever situation you find yourself in.

This is one of the most inherently misunderstood principles in human dynamics. You are always at choice. This means that in essence, you are always autonomous. You get to decide what action you'll take—and what attitude you'll take it with. Own the truth of choice and your need for autonomy will be greatly supported.

• *Maintain Independence.* When you are independent, you are self-governing. You assume responsibility for your life and your choices. Tactics that support a state of independence include earning an income that meets your living expenses, reserving the right to drive yourself to and from meetings or social gatherings, and continually improving your competence by taking on new challenges. This doesn't mean that you won't develop interdependent relationships with others. As we just discovered, we all need other people to meet our need for connection. It does mean that you will assume responsibility to manage your life and work and that you will engage with others out of a genuine desire to connect versus a desperation to be rescued.

• *Commit Consciously.* Many of your most amazing life experiences will come about as a result of your willingness to make a commitment. You must commit yourself before you can establish a strong marriage or become a parent. Your professional success is dependent upon your willingness to commit to your profession, your industry, and your company. Carefully considered and consciously made commitments will support you in living your best life.

Conversely, hastily made commitments can significantly diminish your ability to feel free. Make social commitments only with people you like and enjoy. Volunteer for only those projects that you have a sincere desire to be involved in. Always reserve the right to say *no*! Your willingness to commit yourself only to those people, projects, and events that feel good to you will result in feelings of personal liberation and freedom.

Do you identify with any of these strategies? Are you currently using positive tactics to manage your need for freedom? Do you have any unconscious commitments you may need to get out of? (Most of us do!)

Invest a few moments in evaluating your current approach and determine where you might improve on your existing strategies. The need for autonomy can be incredibly empowering provided it is consciously managed.

The Need to Feel Competent

The requirement of competence combines the need to believe in yourself with the desire to have others believe in you. You must believe that you are capable of producing the results you want in your life and work, and it's important that you feel those around you share your belief.

Your ability to feel personally competent is impacted by the knowledge you possess and the success you've experienced. The knowledge component is situational. Knowing how to do something provides you with a sense of certainty about the process you must follow to accomplish the task at hand. This allows you to feel confident. In instances where you don't have the necessary know-how, an important first step will be acquiring that information.

A more universal factor in feeling competent relates to your level of successful life experience. We all have an experience bank—a collection of memories we can refer to that demonstrate our competence. If you compile an inventory of positive experiences in your bank, your belief in your ability to create what you want grows. This is a self-perpetuating cycle—meaning the more success you experience, the more competent you feel. It can also work in the reverse. When you build up a bank of failed experiences, those memories can undermine your confidence and make you feel incompetent.

Most people feel incredibly uncomfortable when learning a new skill or going for a goal in unfamiliar territory. The nature of a new situation combines the absence of know-how and the lack of an inventory of successful experiences, which is enough to stop some people in their tracks. The most effective way to shore up your confidence includes accessing the information you need to establish your know-how and referring to the successful experiences you've had in other areas of your life.

It is natural to seek external validation from those around you. In fact, your need to receive recognition from others can be a powerfully motivating factor that contributes to your success in life. Typically, the strategies you've developed to meet your need for this external validation will be closely (if not directly) related to the behaviors you've been repeatedly acknowledged for throughout your life. For example, if you've been given attention for your intellect, it is likely you'll work very hard to learn and demonstrate what you know. If you were reinforced for your attractiveness, you'll focus on your beauty. If others recognized you for your humor, you will move heaven and earth to be funny.

As you can imagine, the need to be competent has a profound effect on your personality and your quality of life. It's important to consciously connect with the tactics you use to meet this need, and even more imperative that you ensure they are empowering you. I've provided some examples for you to consider below.

• *Embrace Knowledge.* The more you know about the topic at hand, the more confident you will feel. Invest yourself in learning. If you're trying a new sport or visiting a new location, acquaint yourself with basic information about your new experience. Commit yourself to continually expanding your knowledge in areas that interest you and be willing to do some research before you go into new situations. Information is power! Do your homework at all times. Arm yourself with the facts, and your need for competence will be greatly supported.

• *Actively Accomplish.* You have a lot to contribute to this world. You possess talents and strengths that are unique to you. Nurture and apply these attributes! Shrinking from hard work, hesitating to make a focused effort, and failing to apply yourself breed self-contempt. When you clearly decide what you want to accomplish and you begin to take action toward the achievement of those goals, your self-confidence will go up exponentially. Not only will you satisfy your need for competence, you'll begin to create a fabulous life!

• *Focus on Progress.* Things won't always happen on the timetable you'd like them to. In fact, I guarantee you'll run into problems and delays as you begin to apply yourself. Keep your eye on the progress ball. Give yourself credit for the steps you're taking and the progress you're making. Don't beat yourself up when a bump in the road knocks you down. Rather, pick yourself up, take stock of how much progress you've already made, and start walking again. The habit of focusing on progress will continually fill your experience bank with positive references, which will support your need to feel competent.

• *Embrace Recognition.* It is natural to crave acknowledgement, appreciation, and validation. We all want to be noticed for our accomplishments and contributions. I'm always surprised when I watch a woman shrug off the recognition she receives for a job well done. Don't do that! When someone gives you a compliment, don't just accept it—take it to heart! Allow the full weight of the person's praise to permeate your head and your heart. Then smile, and say *thank you.*

Think back to a time when you felt unstoppably capable. What factors were at play? Did you relate to any of the strategies we've just discussed? Did any of them feel like they might be fun to try? Pick at least one strategy, from those we've discussed or from your own memories, and begin flexing your competence muscles.

The Need to Feel Worthy

I believe the need to feel worthy is the most predominantly debilitating requirement in today's society. It is also the desire that is least often addressed or satisfied.

Let me start by saying: *You are perfect just as you are.* I'd like to say that one more time. *You are perfect, just as you are.* Are you able to accept that statement, or do you resist it? Does it bring tears to your eyes? That's not uncommon. I've met very few women who had full faith in their own worthiness. Those who have possessed that self-assurance have done so only after much soul searching and self-care.

Every situation you've lived through has made you the person you are today, and there is purpose to your experience. While it's true there is room for improvement in all of our lives, the most damaging thoughts you can buy into are those that tell you that you're broken and must fix yourself. That's just not true. You are not broken and, while we can all benefit from self-improvement and self-care, there is nothing about you that needs to be fixed.

It's probable you encountered conditional acceptance as a child. I've *never* encountered anyone who didn't. You could have had these experiences at home, at school, or within your community. As you matured, you learned that you would be accepted *if* you followed the rules of those you sought acceptance from. At home, you may have been required to follow your parents' rules. At school, your teacher had a list of expectations for your behavior, and your classmates likely had rules of their own.

When you were accepted by the people in each of these environments, you learned that you were okay. Each time you experienced rejection or were punished, you learned that a part of you was not acceptable. This process taught you that you were only conditionally worthy.

Were you ever told that you were a bad girl? Each time you heard those words, your feeling of worthiness was diminished. Were you ever told that you weren't special enough to be part of a group, such as the popular crowd at school? Again, each rejection reduced your sense of worthiness.

If you received enough of these messages throughout your life, which is quite common, your belief in your deservingness likely needs to be improved upon.

I have seen so many individuals struggle with deeply held questions related to their personal value. These individuals, driven to prove their worth, have pursued success at any cost—amassing substantial material wealth, achieving high social stature, and excelling in specialized skills, only to find that nothing they accomplish fills the empty hole in their spirit. Ultimately, these individuals sought an external source to tell them that they were okay. Yet, no matter how much external validation they received, they weren't able to accept acknowledgement because they didn't personally believe in their own value.

I want more than that for you! You can take control of your feelings of worth and increase your sense of personal value. I've highlighted several strategies below for you to consider.

• *Invest in Self-Care.* Your willingness to dedicate your time and financial resources to taking care of yourself will directly affect your feelings of worth. Many women have told me that they avoid doing nice things for themselves because it makes them feel selfish. I don't buy it. If you really want to live a selfless life, you will take such great care of yourself that your life force will positively impact every person you come into contact with. Who would you rather be around, the woman who hasn't showered all day, didn't take time to dress herself with care, and drags around like the weight of the world is on her shoulders, or the woman who walks into a room with a vibrant energy, evidently pulled together, and her head held high?

Please hear me now. One of the most selfish acts in life is self-martyrdom. Don't do it. The best thing you can do for your family, friends, colleagues, and community is take great care of *you*. When you are at your best, you can give your best. When you invest in taking great care of yourself, you show your mind, body, heart, and soul how valuable you are. This directly meets your need to feel worthy.

• *Live Up to Your Potential.* Your potential is limitless. You can make contributions to this world that no one else can make. If you don't make them, the world will never see them. In our next step, I'm going to challenge you to explore your potential. For now, I'm going to challenge you to own it.

I see so many women hold themselves back from the true expression of their brilliance. Somewhere along the way, many of us were taught to level the playing field. Did you ever hear phrases such as, "Don't be too smart, or your friends will be threatened," "Don't be too pretty, or the other girls will be jealous," or "Don't be too outspoken, or the boys won't like you"? I know I did.

These types of messages taught you to hold back. I'm challenging you to stop holding back and start being magnificent! The more fully you allow yourself to come into your own, the more fully your need to feel worthy will be met.

• *Speak Up for Yourself.* The manner in which you allow others to interact with you directly impacts your feelings of worth and deservingness. Require that others speak to you with respect. In instances when you encounter someone who is not treating you appropriately, let him or her know that you're not okay with his or her behavior.

Do not allow others to pawn their garbage off on you. You don't need to be running your mother-in-law's errands, and you don't need to listen to your girlfriend whine about the same old problem each time you talk with her. Be willing to say *no*. Be willing to graciously brainstorm alternative ways that your mother-in-law can take care of her errands, or suggest to your girlfriend that you talk about something else. Decide that you are going to establish a set of standards that will govern the way you'll allow others to treat you and a series of boundaries that you'll use when others violate your standards.

Every time you stand up for yourself, you're meeting your need for worthiness.

• *Keep the Commitments You Make to Yourself.* Your feelings of worth are directly affected by your level of self-trust. You must have the ability to rely on your own word, or you will constantly question your own value and deservingness. Think carefully about what you commit to, and make sure that you're making a promise you can keep. If you aren't sure, don't make the promise! Once you make a commitment, do whatever you can to meet it. If circumstances prevent you from following through as promised, make sure to refine and meet your commitment as soon as possible.

Every time you meet a commitment to yourself, you increase your feelings of worth and deservingness. Every time you fail to meet a commitment, you undermine these very needs. Commit carefully, and keep your promises.

Which of these strategies will you embrace? Select one or two and begin experimenting with tactics to meet your need to feel worthy.

PUT IT IN NEUTRAL

Your needs are neutral. They become positive or negative only to the extent that they serve you. If you currently use strategies that help you get more of what you want, those are positive strategies. In instances where you have adopted methods that detract from your life experience, you have the opportunity to improve them.

We all do the best we can with what we know. Perhaps you have not used entirely positive strategies to meet your needs. That's okay. Most people are in the same boat. Now that you know more, your best will improve. Be compassionate with yourself as you move through this portion of the material. You are only human, and the very nature of humanity is imperfect!

CALL TO ACTION – SATISFY YOUR NEEDS

Define the methods you've adopted to satisfy each of the five primary needs.

1. Identify at least one empowering and one disempowering behavior related to each need.
2. Select one of your needs to begin working with. Consider how you might make the disempowering need more positive. How could you shift your approach while still meeting your need?
3. As you master this first need, move to the next of the five primary needs and consider how you might improve upon the strategy you've adopted in that area. Commit to integrating this improvement into your life as well.
4. Follow this process until you've addressed all five needs. It's fine for you to take as little as one week or as much as one month to address each need.

As you begin to approach your life with the intention to integrate your new strategies, you will have opportunities to apply them. The more consistently you apply them, the more natural they'll become.

Wrapping It Up

You are responsible for managing your behavior. One way to do this is to identify and satisfy your needs. No one else in your life is responsible for doing this for you. Your mate can't fill you up. Neither can your children or your job. Until you assume the responsibility to manage and meet your own needs, no amount of love, attention, acceptance, recognition, or validation will have the capacity to make you happy.

Take responsibility for your life and accept the opportunity to create an integrated personal structure that invites, expects, and inspires your personal best. While this process may not be easy, it is inherently valuable. You've been shown a glimpse of what makes you tick—now open your arms to the opportunity to wind your own clock!

BELIEFS

A belief is a firmly held opinion. While your needs drive your behavior, your beliefs color your world. They dictate how you assign meaning and govern your expectations, either limiting or expanding your life possibilities. Ultimately, they define what you hold as truth, which significantly impacts your behavior and your emotional wellness.

Like the strategies you use to satisfy your needs, your beliefs form throughout your life. You learn from every interaction with family, authority figures, classmates, co-workers, and society. As a result, unless you have invested in closely evaluating and refining your belief system, it's likely your structure has been inherited from many of the individuals and experiences from your past.

Once the seed of a belief is planted, your brain collects life experiences to back it up, forming an intellectual repository of proof. Consider a kitchen table. Your beliefs form the top of the table, and the life experiences you've collected as proof of that belief form the table's legs. Your brain moves through this entire process automatically and, in large part, unconsciously.

This is incredibly effective when working with empowering beliefs. Let's say you were told from a very early age that you could accomplish anything you set your mind to. Let's imagine that your parents encouraged you to try new things and frequently reminded you that commitment, information, and hard work would help you create any result you dreamed of. Under these circumstances, you would have amassed a large inventory of accomplishments over the course of your childhood, filling your mental inventory with proof of your competence. As an adult, you would be incredibly confident about tackling new challenges and might even look for opportunities to do so. You would believe in your capability and happily go for your dreams. The core belief that you could accomplish anything with commitment, information, and hard work would generate a self-perpetuating cycle of success throughout your life.

Taking the opposite example, let's suppose your parents told you that you were not that smart and that you couldn't get anything right. With this kind of message, it's likely you wouldn't have applied yourself as forcefully as you could have throughout your childhood. You would have doubted yourself, and this self-doubt and lack of focus would have created an inventory of mediocre performance and unmet goals. It's likely your adulthood would then be filled with more of the same, creating a reality that wouldn't even closely resemble your dreams. The belief that you couldn't get anything right, forged in childhood, would encourage you to settle for the life you'd been presented with versus the life you wanted to live. This failure would then further cement the table legs of belief in your own incompetence, creating a self-fulfilling cycle of failure.

This cycle is critical to evaluate. What you hold as true becomes your reality. Empowering beliefs support your ability to create and appreciate a high quality of life. They help you see possibility and cause you to expect good things to happen. Their negative counterparts, on the other hand, will almost assuredly limit your life experience, causing you to expect the worst and invest your energy in fear.

There are five belief categories that factor into life satisfaction. They are life, self, people, love, and abundance. I invite you to consider each of these areas and identify places where your beliefs could become more powerful.

LIFE

What do you believe about life? Is it a game, meant to be played and enjoyed? Is it a school, ripe with opportunity for learning? Is it a struggle, filled with hardships and strife? Whatever you believe will dictate the way you approach and experience every day of your existence.

Imagine a person who believes life is a precious gift. Several years ago, Dana had a life-threatening illness. She is healthy now, and grateful for her life. She takes joy in her three children and looks forward to meeting a new man when the time seems right. She was divorced a little more than a year ago and has needed some time to adjust to being a single mom. As she drops off her children at school, she notices the birds in the trees and enjoys the smell of her morning coffee. A great song comes on the radio. She turns it up and sings along as she drives to work. She smiles as she finds an open parking spot near the front of her office building and pulls in, jumping out of her car, and saying hello to co-workers as she makes her way into the office. She has many things on her agenda today and can't wait to get to work.

Now consider Keera, who believes that life is hard and filled with suffering. She has three children and a full-time job. She is recently divorced and filled with anger over the breakup of her marriage. She believes the world is out to get her and finds proof of that every day. She has a hard time pulling herself out of bed, can't quite seem to get her children ready to leave the house, and is annoyed by the morning traffic. When she gets to the office, she runs into a cheery co-worker and wonders when the other women will get a grip on reality. Really, there's nothing to be so happy about. She sits down at her computer with a heavy sigh and focuses on getting through the day.

Which of these two women would you rather be around? Which do you most resemble? While you may not have the ability to control all the circumstances of your life, you are solely responsible for managing what things mean to you. You can choose to empower yourself with positive messages, looking for the good in each day, or you can invest yourself in a defeatist attitude. Whatever you choose to believe, you will be right— because your beliefs become your reality.

How long has it been since you've stopped to consider what being alive means to you? Are you like Dana, taking joy in each day? Or are you more like Keera, struggling to make it through the day? Which of your life beliefs limits you? Which opens your world up to possibility? Where might you need to make a shift?

SELF

Do you believe you're a good person? Are you willing to be authentic in your interactions with others, expecting to be accepted? Do you see yourself as intelligent and capable? Are you confident that you can accomplish the goals you set out to achieve?

Are you unsure of yourself? Do you believe you're flawed in some way? Are you still carrying those messages within you about what a "bad girl" you are? Do you doubt your ability to impact your life, making changes once you commit to something?

Your self-beliefs dictate what you will attempt and how fully you'll allow yourself to participate in life. They govern how much love you will allow yourself to receive and the quality of connection you're able to establish with others. A conviction in your own goodness and capacity for accomplishment acts as a grounding foundation for your existence, allowing you to pursue your dreams and create rich relationships. Conversely, buying into beliefs that you're not smart enough, not capable enough, or flawed in some way undermines your ability to stand strong in your being.

When you believe there is something wrong with you, your energy will be invested in hiding this truth. You'll live in fear, not joy. You'll avoid getting close to others, because you'll fear their reaction once they get to know the real you, and you'll avoid pursuing your dreams out of a secret fear that you'll fail and be found out for the fraud you fear you are.

You must establish a solid belief in your goodness, deservingness, and competence in order to stand strong in life. As you make the investment in developing and nurturing empowering self-beliefs, you will experience a new vitality, which you can then channel into creating success, happiness, and fulfillment.

What do you believe about yourself? Are you competent? Are you a good person who deserves great things? What do you fear about yourself? Where are you holding yourself back? Where might you need to shift your beliefs?

PEOPLE

The truth you hold about people governs your interaction with them. Do you believe people are kind, or do you think they'll hurt you? Do you have specific beliefs about men, women, or people of a certain race or culture?

The authenticity within you knows that people do the best they can with what they know. She believes in the goodness and equality of people and knows we're all connected and looking for the same things in life— love, acceptance, fulfillment, meaning, comfort, and a sense of purpose.

There is another part of you, based in fear, that distrusts people's motives and encourages you to protect yourself from getting too close to others. She causes you to question those who look or think differently from you and invites you to separate yourself from others, focusing on your differences rather than your commonality.

Which of these two influences will you allow to dictate your reality? When you believe in the goodness of people, you open yourself to true intimacy. When you allow fear to reside over your beliefs, you'll likely invest your emotional energy in protecting yourself. It's very difficult to develop and nurture a genuine bond when part of you is posturing for safety. Ultimately, this undermines your ability to meet your need for connection and leads to feelings of isolation and loneliness.

What do you believe about people? Do you trust yourself to bring good people into your life? Do you trust those in your life to do the right thing? Where might you need to improve upon your truths?

LOVE

This is a loaded one. Do you believe you're lovable? In your mind, is there such a thing as soul mates? What has your experience with commitment taught you about marriage and relationships?

The experiences you had as a child formed your love beliefs. First and foremost, the way you received love in your early years will dictate what makes you feel most loved today. If you grew up in an affectionate family, it's probable you'll associate feelings of love to physical demonstrations of affection, such as hugging, cuddling, kissing, and handholding. If your family was very expressive and communicated feelings of love through words, you may feel most loved when you're told that you are. Conversely, if you received no such messages as a child, you may doubt your own lovability.

If you grew up with a parental model of a healthy marriage, you probably developed empowering beliefs about relationships. These beliefs might dictate the roles each partner should play in the union, such as the division of household and financial duties and the manner in which the inevitability of conflict is managed. If you grew up with an unhealthy or dysfunctional marriage model, it's likely you'll question the value of marriage or the possibility of happy-couple-dom. Being that most of us did not grow up learning from a happy marriage model, it's possible your beliefs can be improved upon in this area.

Building upon your experiences, both your beliefs about yourself and other people factor into this equation. If you believe you are good and worthy of love, you will be much more likely to attract healthy people into your life and expect a high standard of treatment from them. Your faith in people will cause you to look for the genuine goodness in each person in your life, and this will allow you to have high-quality connections.

Conversely, if you have doubts about your own deservingness of love or you mistrust people, you probably have some unhealthy beliefs about love and relationships. These beliefs could cause you to live in fear of abandonment or prompt you to be suspicious of your partner. Not only is this environment detrimental to building a quality union, it can wreak havoc on your emotional stability.

Consider the love models you experienced as you grew up. Invest a few moments in evaluating what makes you feel loved and how the beliefs you hold about yourself, people, and relationships impact your love connections. Where might you make an improvement?

ABUNDANCE

Do you believe there is enough wealth and success to go around? Do you think that people who have a lot in their lives must be dishonest or must have to work harder than you're willing to work? Have you invested yourself in the false notion that for you to win someone else has to lose?

Your beliefs about abundance determine what you're willing to go for and what you'll allow yourself to have. Typically, these beliefs manifest when talking about money and success. If you hold a belief that wealthy people must be dishonest and don't believe yourself to be dishonest, you will undermine your ability to create wealth. If you think that professionally successful people have to sacrifice their families to be successful and believe it's wrong to do so, you will sabotage your efforts toward professional growth and achievement.

The truth is, life is filled with abundance. There is no shortage of any good thing in this world. Yet, if you grew up with messages about scarcity or witnessed the rejection of accomplished people, it's quite possible you've developed a set of unhealthy beliefs about the availability or consequences of abundance.

What does it take to create financial abundance? What would it take for you to accomplish the goals you hold most dear? Do you associate a negative consequence to either circumstance? Invest yourself in developing a belief set around abundance and watch your world blossom!

CALL TO ACTION – SHIFT YOUR BELIEFS

1. Identify one empowering belief in each of the five belief categories.
2. How has that belief served you in your life and work?
3. Now, identify one disempowering belief in each category.
4. For each belief, ask yourself the following:
   - Identify it – Write the belief down.
   - Define it – What is holding your tabletop up? What experiences are you using to prove the belief?
   - Disprove it – Are your proof points really valid? What else could they mean?
   - Shift it – How could you improve upon this belief, so that it serves you? What proof points could you use for your new table legs?

Here's an example from one of my clients.
   - Identify it – Karen believed she was too young to apply for a promotion she was very interested in.
   - Define it – She'd been told by her supervisor that her youth would work against her in the application process and that she should commit to getting several more years of experience under her belt before attempting to move up the ranks.
   - Disprove it – As she examined her life experience, Karen realized she was always a little bit ahead of the curve in her growth and development. She had skipped a grade in school, was the first of her peers to drive, and had completed college one semester early.

- Shift it – Karen decided that buying into her original belief was not serving her. She realized that her youth could add a great deal of value to the current management team, infusing the group with new energy and perspective. She created a list of things that her youth would allow her to contribute and read through them to firmly put her table legs in place. Several weeks later, Karen was awarded the promotion.

Wrapping It Up

What you hold as truth becomes your reality. Don't place limits on your success or hold yourself back from your dreams. Instead, use the power of your beliefs to support you in the pursuit of fulfilling work and a happy life.

KEY LEARNING POINTS

• Your basic human needs for security, connection, autonomy, competence, and worthiness drive your behavior.

• These needs are neutral. They become positive or negative based on the quality of the strategies used to meet them.

• When you proactively develop strategies to meet your needs, you put yourself in control of your behavior. When you don't, your needs control you.

• Your beliefs are firmly held opinions that dictate how you assign meaning to your life experiences. Beliefs about life, self, people, love, and abundance color your day-to-day reality, either limiting or expanding your world.

• Strategies for satisfying beliefs and needs are formed in early childhood and conditioned throughout your life. They are related to the experiences you've had with parents, authority figures, classmates, co-workers, and society.

• You can shift any belief and improve any need's satisfaction strategy by using the formulas within this chapter.

STEP 4

LIGHT YOUR FIRE: THE PASSION TRIAD

How long has it been since you took on the day with unbridled enthusiasm? Can you recall the last time you experienced intense excitement or pure joy? Are you a passionate person? If so, what are you passionate about? If not, are you ready to heat things up?

We all want to feel passion—that intensely charged arousal that makes our heart beat faster and causes us to lose track of time. In fact, one of the first things many of my coaching clients want to accomplish is to reconnect with their passion and purpose.

This powerful feeling is caused by your heart's recognition that you are in the midst of something native to your authentic self. In essence, your passion is ignited when you reconnect with what you were made to do and who you were made to be. The intense joy associated with living passionately is a direct result of living authentically.

In childhood, we are filled with passion. We are also closer to our authentic selves than at any other time in our lives. Have you ever watched a young child go about his or her day? Whatever task the child undertakes—whether it's playing a game or watching a movie—he or she throws his or her whole being into it. Children are not self-conscious, and they know instinctively what will give them maximum pleasure. Not only are they aware of what they want, they're willing to go for it! They haven't been taught to hold themselves back, to behave appropriately, or to contain their enthusiasm.

Adults, on the other hand, have learned all of those lessons. You've been taught to play it cool, to contain your natural emotions in order to appear rational, and to approach your life practically and realistically.

I would love to throw the word *realistic* out of the English language! Realism leads to repression, and if you're repressed you're not feeling passionate. The good news is even sleeping passion can be awakened. In Step 4, that's what we're going to do—awaken yours.

How do you rouse and reconnect with those feelings of attraction, interest, infatuation, anticipation, and enthusiasm? You claim your strengths, integrate your values, and step into your purpose.

CLAIM YOUR STRENGTHS

What qualities do you respect and admire in yourself? What characteristics do others acknowledge you for? What are you naturally good at? Your strengths are the natural abilities or aptitudes that are unique to you. They are generally expressed in terms of describing your personality or capability. For example, you're smart, you're witty, you're a great athlete, or you're artistic.

One of the biggest mistakes people make in the area of personal development is placing their focus on their weaknesses. For some reason, many people have bought into the notion that most of their energy should be directed at shoring up inadequacies in their talent, knowledge, or skill base. What these people don't realize is that when you invest in developing your natural gifts, the simple power of those attributes eclipses your weaknesses.

I'm not suggesting that you avoid acknowledging your personal shortcomings or shy away from learning new skills or information. I am reminding you that no one is good at everything, yet everyone is good at something! The first step in awakening and unleashing your passion involves committing your focus to the naming and claiming of your strengths.

These abilities are actually hardwired in your brain. Quite literally, you are born to be good at specific things, and we are each born with a unique presence and combination of specific attributes. Rather than attempting to reverse your biology, why not invest in maximizing the gifts you've been given?

Have you ever had a job interview where the interviewer asked you to describe your best qualities? That's exactly how we'll begin to identify your strengths.

CALL TO ACTION – PART ONE: NAME YOUR STRENGTHS

In this exercise, I invite you to write down your ten greatest strengths. You can identify these qualities on your own, borrow from the list of possible strengths I've provided below, or ask two or three people close to you to tell you what they believe your strengths are. (Make sure you only ask positive, supportive people for this kind of help!) Now is not the time to be modest. It is time to toot your own horn. Have fun with this exercise! What are your greatest strengths?

Adventurous	Fair
Analytical	Friendly
Artistic	Get results
Athletic	Great presenter
Beautiful	High integrity
Charismatic	Honest
Communicate well	Humble
Compassionate	Humorous
Considerate	Influential
Courageous	Innovative
Creative	Inspiring
Determined	Intelligent
Enthusiastic	Kind

Knowledgeable
Likable
Listen well
Loving
Make things happen
Open
Optimistic
Organized
Original
Patient
Peaceful
Persistent
Persuasive
Practical
Problem solver

Procedure-oriented
Punctual
Resilient
Responsible
Sensible
Steadfast
Stylish
Supportive
Talented
Teacher
Trusting
Trustworthy
Visionary
Warm
Wise

Now summarize your findings.
My greatest strengths are:

_____
_____
_____
_____
_____
_____
_____
_____
_____

Now that you've named your strengths, it's time to claim them. When you claim your natural abilities, you step into them. You own them. This allows you to consciously begin cultivating them.

CALL TO ACTION – PART TWO: CLAIM YOUR STRENGTHS

For each of the strengths you've identified, recall at least one accomplishment or contribution you've made as a result of using that strength. If you can think of more than one example, that's great. At a minimum, identify one example for each of your strengths. You can come up with these on your own, or ask someone close to you for help.

Wrapping It Up

Claiming your strengths is the first factor in the passion triad. As you become clear about your gifts, you will naturally seek opportunities to apply them. This action pulls you into a cycle of success, with each strength-based accomplishment contributing priceless deposits to your self-confidence account. This shift, in and of itself, is incredibly powerful. You make it even more profound when you add the second factor in the passion triad—your values.

INTEGRATE YOUR VALUES

I'm always careful about the discussion of values because so much of our culture equates them with a sense of morality. In the coaching world, values are referred to as those qualities or interests that you're naturally drawn to. They're the realities of life you truly appreciate and are key markers along the road to passion.

When you reconnect with the emotions that are innately and excitingly important to you, your world becomes rich and your purpose becomes clear. You begin to approach life differently, and you respond to situations with greater perspective. You set goals with more clarity and embrace success with an enhanced level of happiness, acceptance, and appreciation.

EMOTIONAL CLUES

Before you can reconnect with your passion, you must re-establish your ability to feel. In most cases, we live life in our heads. We think everything through and attempt to rationally uncover the answers to our questions, paying little attention to our emotions. The problem with this approach is that your passion will be revealed to you through your feelings, not your thoughts.

How do you rediscover your emotional experience? You begin paying attention to the signals you get from your body. Perhaps when you're excited you get a tingle up your spine or an acceleration of your heartbeat. You might feel butterflies in your stomach or a tickle in your throat. Everyone experiences feelings differently, but we all *always* encounter some physical sensation along with our emotions.

CALL TO ACTION – IDENTIFY YOUR PASSION SIGNALS

Sit quietly and comfortably for a few moments. Focus on the movement of your breath in and out of your body. Consciously take three deep breaths. Think back to a time when you felt incredibly passionate. This can be a recent experience or a situation from your past. Put yourself back in that place. What sensations do you feel in your body? Do you feel energized? Are you feeling a specific part of your body? Make note of the feelings you're experiencing. These are your body's signals that you have entered the vicinity of your passion. These signals will guide you as you continue in your exploration.

If you aren't able to remember a passionate experience or can't feel any sensation in your body, that's okay. Move forward with the remaining exercises and consider coming back to this activity once you've completed the chapter.

THE POWER OF ATTRACTION

When you are attracted to something or someone, you become interested, animated, possibly even captivated. This magnetic pull provides you with important clues as to the values that will awaken your passion. You will be naturally drawn to experiences that incorporate the essence of your values. Discovering these natural attraction markers is your next step. Let's get started.

What Do You Like to Read?

When you enter a bookstore, what section do you head to first? Is there an area in the library you can easily get lost in? Look at your bookshelves. Do you typically buy one kind of book?

Which magazines do you look forward to receiving and reading each month? Do you skip to specific sections in those magazines when they arrive? The interest you have in the subject matter or theme of your reading materials can be very telling.

If you gravitate toward the self-help section of the bookstore and your favorite magazines have to do with self-improvement, it's possible you value learning, growth, discovery, and transformation.

The way to know for sure is to ask yourself what you love about the kind of books you prefer. What is it about your favorite magazine that most interests you? The essence of your pleasure is related to what you value, and your values are the second factor in the passion triad.

How Do You Like to Be Entertained?

Do you love a specific kind of movie? What kind of television programming do you prefer? What do you TIVO or program your VCR to tape when you're away? Would you be thrilled to attend a sporting event, or does a play sound more to your liking? Do you enjoy being active in the great outdoors, or does the hustle and bustle of a big city enthrall you?

Your preferences are powerful clues. An interest in comedies could reflect values such as laughing, being funny, happiness, and humor.

Interest in nature could indicate a value set of adventure, fitness, nature, beauty, or spirituality.

What is the essence of your preferences? Again, it's the core element of your choices that tell the story of your values. Take a moment to break down your selections and uncover more clues to your passion.

What Are Your Favorite Pastimes?

If you had one free day where everything on your to-do list would get done and everyone in your family would be taken care of, what would you do? Would you spend the day poolside reading a good book? Would you cook a gourmet meal, or go antiquing? Would you spend the afternoon with people you care about, or would you enjoy a morning at the gym and an afternoon at the spa?

Once you've determined what you'd do, decide why that would be satisfying. What about those activities interests you? For example, if you'd prefer to spend the day with friends, it might be that you really appreciate the connection and communication you give and receive in this situation. If being at the gym and taking a spa day sounded heavenly, it could be that health, fitness, solitude, or beauty is part of your value set.

When Do You Feel Most Natural?

When are you the most natural and at ease? Is there something you do that others recognize you for, yet you feel it's so effortless that you have a hard time accepting praise for it? Think back to what you discovered in the personal strengths exercise earlier in this chapter. Your inherent abilities will provide you with additional clues about your values.

My husband and I have a ranch in Washington State. It's bordered on one side by a fly-fishing river and on the other by a 30-acre horse pasture. During our last visit, our family wanted to go for a trail ride. It was a beautiful summer morning, and I remember smiling as I watched my husband and brother-in-law head into the field to catch the horses for our ride.

Anyone who has ever been around horses knows that if a horse doesn't want to be ridden it can be pretty tough to catch. Being that these horses were roaming free on thirty acres of open field, I didn't expect the guys to successfully bring the animals into the barn anytime soon.

Then the most amazing thing happened. My brother-in-law had brought his new Blue Tick Healer puppy with him to our place. These dogs are herding animals. It's in their essential nature to round up animals. Blue, as he's called, ran out to the field with the guys. As soon as they got close to the horses, this four-month-old puppy went to work. In a matter of moments he had all of the horses in the corral near our barn.

This was one of the most powerful demonstrations of the principle of passion I'd ever seen. This little dog had never received any training. He'd only been away from his mother for a matter of weeks, yet he had enthusiastically gone to work *doing what he was made to do.*

You were made to do the things you are naturally good at. They are part of your DNA. For example, if you effortlessly order projects or environments you may value organization. If you easily spend quiet time with yourself, solitude or self-connection could be very important to you. If creating something where nothing existed before thrills you, building or manifestation could be part of your value structure.

Nature has purpose, and it's manifested in your natural abilities. The more closely you align with these traits and the values at their essence, the more likely you are to experience great passion and fulfillment.

What Could You Teach?

Do you have great knowledge about a specific subject? Have you ever been told that you should write a book or teach a class? What would that book or class be about? The things you are drawn to spend time learning about and discussing with others are related to your values.

I worked in Corporate America for ten years before becoming a coach. I love business, so I enjoyed my experience most of the time. On "the side," I read book after book about self-development. I went to ten or fifteen seminars per year, and I worked with my own coach. I loved talking with others about human development, and I invested great amounts of my time and energy into mentoring and training my staff. I was naturally gravitating toward one of my highest values—growth.

Consider what the core elements of your interests are. What about your favorite subject is so intriguing to you? Any subject you have an affinity for is likely related to your values.

What Brings You Joy?

Does the early morning sunshine make you happy? Do you love peach roses, the smell of lavender, or the feel of your pet's fur? Is the deliciousness of a hot, scented bath heaven to you? Are you grateful for the quiet moments you get to spend snuggling in the warmth of your partner's arms?

Joy is an authentic emotion. It emanates from the core of your being in response to the recognition that you are satisfying the deepest desires of your heart. When you fill your life with things you genuinely adore and appreciate, you infuse your being with an overwhelming sense of contentment and peace. I'm sure you've experienced those moments when everything seemed right in your world, and your recognition of this rightness caused emotion to well up in your spirit. This is pure joy.

The things that bring you joy are likely linked to your values. If you cherish the experience of being tucked under a cozy blanket with a great book, you might value solitude, self-connection, or the adventure unfolding in your novel. If you love animals, you could value nature, unconditional love, or loyalty.

Reconnecting with the things that bring you joy infuses your life with meaning, bringing you back to the realization that every moment of every day is ripe with possibility for passionate happiness.

CALL TO ACTION – PART ONE: CREATE YOUR ATTRACTION PROFILE

It's time to create your attraction profile. Set aside fifteen to twenty minutes to answer the following questions.

- What do you like to read?
- How do you like to be entertained?
- What are your favorite pastimes?
- When do you feel most natural?
- What could you teach?
- What brings you joy?
- For each of your discoveries, define the essence of what you identified.
- Summarize your findings. These will likely become part of your core values or will be closely related to them.

CALL TO ACTION – PART TWO: IDENTIFY YOUR CORE VALUES

In the next part of this exercise, I've provided you with a list of words that are commonly found on value lists. Identify the words that jump out at you. Pay special attention to words that resemble or duplicate the essence you identified in the first part of this exercise. The list is quite long, so try to limit your selections to no more than ten words. You'll need fifteen to twenty minutes for this exercise.

Accomplishment	Confident
Adventurous	Connection
Artistic	Contribute
Beautiful	Creative
Bold	Dependable
Cared-for	Detailed
Caring	Discovery
Catalyze	Effective
Charitable	Efficient
Cheerful	Empathic
Communication	Empowered
Compassionate	Energetic
Competitive	Enlightened

Extroverted	Open-minded
Faithful	Optimistic
Family	Orderly
Fit	Organized
Flexible	Original
Friendship	Patient
Fun	Peaceful
Funny	Planning
Gratitude	Play
Growth	Pleasure
Happiness	Positive
Healthy	Potential
Helpful	Powerful
Honest	Progressive
Humble	Relatedness
Humorous	Resilient
Impactful	Reverent
Influential	Self-care
Inspirational	Self-connection
Intelligent	Sensitive
Introverted	Sensual
Inventive	Sexy
Kind	Simplicity
Leader	Spirituality
Learn	Student
Loving	Teach
Loyal	Thrifty
Magical	Transformation
Magnetic	Travel
Manifestation	Trustworthy
Musical	Truth
Nurturing	Visionary

Wealthy   Witty

Win   Worldly

Wise

Now, summarize your findings.

My Core Values Structure:

_____

_____

_____

_____

_____

_____

_____

_____

_____

_____

CLIENT PROFILE – LAURA

Laura was a delightful, funny, warm woman in her late thirties. She hired me to help her reconnect with her passion and define a mission for her life. She had recently left the corporate world, after investing seventeen years in her chosen industry. She didn't know what she wanted to do, but she knew it wasn't what she'd been doing up to this point. As we got started, I asked her to talk with me about her greatest strengths. For a moment she appeared surprised, then began to talk in a hesitant voice. I stopped her early into our discussion and asked her where her hesitancy was coming from. She explained that she'd always been told not to brag, and she didn't want to seem boastful in our discussions.

I assured her that the purpose of our discussion was to define her gifts and reminded her that we would not have the ability to uncover her purpose unless and until she was willing to own those strengths. With resolve she began again, and we continued our discussion focused on defining both her strengths and values.

For her homework, I asked Laura to talk with five people who knew her well and have them tell her what they perceived to be her five greatest strengths and her five greatest loves. When Laura and I met again, there was a light in her eyes. She told me that all of her friends had referenced three of the same strengths that she had initially identified—her natural organizational skills, her great personal discipline, and her talent for connecting people with one another. When discussing the things Laura loved, two other things continually emerged—her love of art and her joy in being with people.

Over the course of the next two months, we took those factors and applied them to a number of different scenarios. Laura spoke with individuals who were in the midst of the types of careers she was considering. We discussed how she could combine her strengths and gifts in some form of service to her community and, ultimately, Laura found her path.

Three months after we began working together, Laura discovered that she wanted to own an art gallery. Her love of art was pronounced, and she took great joy in connecting people with one another, which was also one of her strengths. Her impeccable organization was a great asset in running a business, and her discipline would be vital along each step of her path.

Laura was thrilled. Today, she owns and operates a wonderful gallery in a coastal California town. She is busy, yet every facet of her day is filled with things she loves. She is using her strengths, embracing her passion, and serving a powerful purpose in her community.

Wrapping It Up

Your values are expressions of your authenticity, and when you make room for them in your life, you ignite your passion. Those smoldering fires burst into joyful flames when you add the last factor in the passion triad—purpose.

STEP INTO YOUR PURPOSE

There are many misconceptions about life purpose in our society. Invariably, people think that finding their purpose means discovering their perfect career—but purpose is so much more than that! Purpose has little to do with *what* you do. It has everything to do with *who* you are and *how* you do everything you do.

Purpose touches every dimension of your life. When you commit to living purposefully, your association with family, friends, co-workers, and your community will shift, and you will view your home, work, finances, and life experiences through new eyes. As a result, things that used to seem frustrating might become interesting. Where you used to feel fear, you will invest your energy in responsible action and faith in the rightness of your experience. Where apathy used to live, passion will course through your veins. You will feel truly alive.

Creating this powerful energy is quite simple. When you combine your natural strengths with your values and offer those gifts to others in the form of service, you step into purposeful living.

THE POWER OF SERVICE

You have been uniquely gifted with a specific combination of aptitudes and a predisposition to special interests and emotions. These are your strengths and your values. When you offer these gifts in the form of service, you make a contribution to your fellow man.

There is no one else like you in the world. Like your DNA, your strengths and values form a structure unique to you. This means that you are uniquely qualified to make a contribution to your world that only you can make.

This contribution need not be complicated. On the contrary, it will be incredibly simple. Let's suppose you identified your strengths as *good listener, clear communicator, detail-oriented,* and *compassionate.* Let's also imagine you discovered that your values were *learning, connection, transformation,* and *love.*

Taking your unique structure into consideration, your gifts could be used in numerous ways. Your ability to be a good listener coupled with your value of connection would make you a wonderful conversationalist. You would naturally create rich, deep, intimate relationships, which would bring joy to you and those who share their lives with you.

Using your skills as a clear communicator along with your love of learning, you could be a powerful teacher. This does not necessarily mean you'd need to be in a classroom. Living purposefully would turn life into your classroom. You could approach each day with an intention to learn something new, share your knowledge, and have meaningful exchanges with others. Think about how much more interesting some of the seemingly mundane tasks in your life would become using this approach.

You are in service when you are adding value. Each day presents you with innumerable opportunities to make contributions to your community. A smile is a simple gift that can warm a heart. Allowing someone to pull in front of you in traffic might allow that person to reach an appointment on time. Remembering to ask the grocery clerk about something she mentioned to you last week could make her feel seen and valued.

This approach is even more powerful with the people closest to you. When you live purposefully, your family is transformed. Can you imagine what kind of child you could raise in an environment of listening, learning, clear communication, and compassion? And what about the impact she might have in the world as a result of being raised in that manner?

Do you remember those Breck television commercials in the early '70s? The commercial would show a beautiful woman with healthy, shiny hair, telling you how much she loved the shampoo. Then she would say something to the effect of "so I told my friend," and the screen would show two women. After that, you would hear an echo of "and she told someone, and she told someone, and so on, and so on," as the women on the screen multiplied.

This is the impact your commitment to living purposefully can have on your world. Your intention to add value using your natural strengths and values becomes a ripple in the pond of change, inviting others to live purposefully too. This is powerful!

LIVING PURPOSEFULLY

Another misconception about life purpose is that it must be related to a huge undertaking, such as discovering a new world, curing the sick, or feeding the hungry. For some people, their unique strengths and values may call them to serve in this way. But for most of us, living purposefully is based on how we approach the routine and seemingly small things we do each day.

Connecting with your purpose does not have to turn your world on its ear. It does not require massive sacrifice or suffering. It simply requires a shift in your perspective, recognition for what has always been within you, and a willingness to offer those gifts in service.

Intention in Action

The key to making this powerful shift rests in your willingness to intentionally apply your strengths and values in service each day. To be intentional is to be deliberate. When you deliberately approach your day, looking for ways to apply and experience your gifts and values, you will be rewarded with a passionate, purposeful life experience, even when you're dealing with difficult issues.

For example, if you value connection, you have the opportunity to turn every encounter with another human being into a satisfying experience. What would happen if you were to approach every interaction with the intention to learn about the people you encountered or to express warmth and friendliness to each person who crossed your path? You would undoubtedly leave each encounter, from the grocery clerk to your co-workers, feeling more connected to your community. And you would leave many smiles and warm feelings with the people you'd made those connections with.

If nurturing is one of your values, you have the opportunity to turn every action you take in caring for your loved ones, from the simplest household tasks to your time spent with them, into a purposefully passionate experience.

While this may seem like a bit of "work" in the moment, the process becomes quite automatic after a short period of time. I liken it to learning how to drive a car with a manual transmission. Initially, you have to think about each individual step involved with shifting gears, but after you've driven for a short time you become incredibly proficient at the mechanics. So it is with an intentional approach to life.

YOUR RECIPE FOR PASSION

Understanding the nuts and bolts of strength, values, and purposeful service will take you more than halfway down the road of passion. You complete your journey when you commit to adopting this intentional approach to living.

Fortunately, completion is very simple. You only need to define your recipe for success and dedicate yourself to creating opportunities to experience your purposeful delicacy each day. Your recipe goes like this: my strengths + my values x service = passionate, purposeful living.

CALL TO ACTION - DEFINE YOUR PASSION TRIAD

In this exercise, we will customize your Recipe for Success and consider specific opportunities for you to begin using this powerful structure.

My Strengths Are:

_____

_____

_____

_____

_____

My Values Are:

_____

_____

_____

_____

To live purposefully, seek opportunities to offer your strengths and values each day. Remember that your offering need not be grand. The power of your passion will be unleashed through simple action. What are some specific opportunities you might have to offer service using your values and strengths?

Ways I Can Offer My Strengths and Gifts in Service:

_____

_____

_____

_____

_____

Wrapping It Up

When you actualize something, you make it a reality. The act of claiming your strengths, integrating your values, and offering your gifts in a purposeful way brings you to the center of your authentic self. In this place, you will not only awaken your once-sleeping passion, you will inflame it. Live passionately!

KEY LEARNING POINTS

• Your passion is ignited when you reconnect with what you were made to do and who you were made to be.

• You can reconnect with your passion when you claim your strengths, integrate your values, and step into your purpose.

• Your strengths are the natural abilities or aptitudes that are unique to you. The first step in awakening and unleashing your passion involves committing your focus to the naming and claiming of your strengths.

• Your values are those qualities or interests that you're naturally drawn to or that you appreciate. Identifying and integrating your values is the second step in re-igniting your passion.

• You begin to live passionately when you intentionally combine your strengths with your values and offer those gifts to others in the form of service each day.

PART
THREE

DEVELOP YOUR DREAM

STAKE YOUR CLAIM: THE LIFE
OF YOUR DREAMS IS WITHIN REACH

D o you live by design or default? How long has it been since you sat down with your dreams and structured your ideal life? Most people never do. Instead, they focus on getting through the day or surviving the week. They react to the circumstances of their lives, feeling a vague sense of dissatisfaction and an overwhelming busyness, which stops them from seriously looking at how they're experiencing each day. As a result, they live by default.

A balanced life is, in essence, a designed life. It is a life that has been clearly crafted, carefully nurtured, and intentionally acted upon. A well-designed life allows its owner to answer key questions such as: What do you want for yourself? What would your ideal day look and feel like? Can you imagine your dream home? Are there key experiences you'd love to have, places you'd like to visit, or people you'd like to meet? What do you want for your family and the quality of relationships you share with others? Finally, what is your calling?

The life of your dreams is *possible* and *within reach*. Anything you can imagine has the potential to become part of your reality, but first you *must imagine it!* The life design process in this step combines the energy of *vision* with the focus of *planning* and the commitment of *action* to breathe life into your dreams.

Whether you've never moved through an exercise of this nature or you regularly take stock of your life, this stage of our process asks you to take a closer look at the way you're living. It helps you establish a clear picture of what you want and challenges you to overcome the common obstacles to a well-designed life.

GETTING CLEAR GIVES YOU POWER

In my work with clients, I've encountered three obstacles that keep people stuck in mediocrity. Typically if one or more of these blocks is present, you're likely to surrender to the life you have instead of working toward the life you want. These common obstacles are learned helplessness, fear, and the absence of a plan.

LIVING IN LEARNED HELPLESSNESS

The theory of learned helplessness states that when an individual lacks belief in her ability to change the circumstances of her life or fears the unknown results of the changes she might make, it becomes easier for her to settle for the life she has than it would be to go for the life she wants. While she may not be truly happy, she is not unhappy enough to do anything about it. Therefore, she remains stuck in a mediocre existence. Does this sound familiar?

Most of us have experienced some element of learned helplessness. Perhaps you aren't totally satisfied with your weight, but you've tried and failed to change your body so many times that you've stopped believing you're capable of reaching your ideal. You could be worried about your credit card balances, yet feel so overwhelmed at the monumental task of paying them down that you resign yourself to living in debt. You could wish for an intimate relationship, yet allow your fear that there are "no good men left" to stop you from looking.

Your focus on how difficult it might be to create the results you want literally immobilizes you, causing you to settle for the status quo.

I liken this surrender to choosing to live in a black-and-white world instead of experiencing a Technicolor existence. Don't you want to live in full color?

Think about any area of your life where you feel a sense of dissatisfaction. Do you believe you're capable of making a change? What are you afraid you'd have to give up in order to change your current circumstances? What do you fear you might risk if you really gave it a shot?

You deserve to live in full, vibrant, extravagant color! Right now, I challenge you to stop settling for the life you have. Instead, commit to creating the life you dream of. Even if you've fallen into learned helplessness, you can self-correct *right now*. Step into your power and decide you're going to go for your dreams.

FEAR OR FAITH?

What are you afraid of? Are you worried you'll make a mistake and create disastrous consequences for yourself? Are you afraid that you won't know the answer to a question and your lack of knowledge may cause others to look down on you? Do you worry about being rejected if you succeed beyond your peers or about being ostracized if you fall short of a goal?

We are all afraid. This is a normal part of life. We fear the unknown, yet the known doesn't always fulfill us. We fear death, yet we also fear life. We fear risking to love yet we're terrified of being alone. We fear failure and are equally concerned about success. Every one of us is afraid. The difference between balanced, successful, fulfilled women and their less satisfied counterparts is based on how they manage their fear. Will you allow fear to stop you, or will you acknowledge and move through it?

Ultimately, the essence of your fears is directly related to the certainty you have about your ability to handle the circumstances you encounter in life. If you fear being abandoned, the essence of your worry is more about your belief in how you would handle being alone than it is about someone leaving your life. If you're terrified of failing to reach a goal, what you're really worried about is how you would handle the reality of falling short of your objectives. In essence, your fear is about you and whether or not you're capable of surviving disappointment, unmet expectations, or possible rejection.

This is a very powerful realization, because while you can't control the actions of other people, you can absolutely control your own. You can shape and mold your self-belief, and you can strengthen your courage muscles. The chief resource in your strengthening arsenal is faith.

Eleanor Roosevelt said, "Courage is not movement in the absence of fear. Courage is movement in the face of fear." The faith you cultivate in your ability to handle whatever circumstances life hands you will provide you with the armor needed to walk through your fear and achieve your dreams.

Faith is simply a strong belief about something. Building your own reservoir of faith is as simple as remembering who you are. What do you know about yourself? Think about the experiences you've endured and the resilience, strength, and resolve you've demonstrated throughout your life. Think about the obstacles you've faced, the contributions you've made, and the things you've achieved. You may never have thought about yourself as a heroic or courageous woman before, but I'll assure you that you are both heroic and courageous.

Monsters live in the dark. When you feel fear, your first move must be to turn the light on. Ask yourself, "What's the worst thing that could happen?" Clearly define your worst-case scenario and consider whether or not you can handle that reality. If you can, stare your misgivings right in the face and move forward. If you can't, consider what circumstances, support, or personal belief you need to develop in order to increase your capacity to handle worst-case circumstances.

In most instances, you'll find that using this approach lessens the enormity of your fear and increases your self-confidence. If you encounter a circumstance you don't believe you can handle, don't beat yourself up.

Simply continue to invest in your own growth and development. Scale your initial goal back, which will mitigate the worst-case potential. Take baby steps that allow you to develop your courage muscles. Then infuse yourself with faith.

Don't let your fears hold you back from having the life you deserve. You are a strong, resilient, capable, courageous, heroic woman, and you can handle whatever life throws you. Take a deep breath, remind yourself of your strength, and gently move forward to claim your dream.

THE POWER IS IN THE PLAN

When you consciously define what you want in every area of your life—in your relationships, with your finances, in your career, with your body, in your home, for your community, and in your personal experience—you increase your odds of life satisfaction. When you combine this clear vision with a structured plan to guide your daily activity, your odds improve yet again. When you add the power of committed action to your vision and plan, you reach a level of almost assured success.

Using a plan directs your energy. It helps you make good choices about where to invest your time and puts the individual components of your life in context. When you take the time to complete your life design and develop a plan to support that vision, your focus becomes clear and you increase your power to stay on course.

Most people fail to create the results they want in their lives because they haven't committed to living by a plan. Instead, they've allowed their fears and busyness to lull them into a settled state of learned helplessness. The good news is *you aren't most people, and you don't have to settle.*

You're poised at a perfect cross section on the road of your life. Will you live by design or default? I challenge you to choose the path of design. The energy, focus, and enthusiasm a plan will unleash in your life will lead you to success beyond your wildest imagination.

CALL TO ACTION – MOVE BEYOND THE COMMON BLOCKS OF MANIFESTATION

Take a few moments to answer the following questions.
1. Have you surrendered to learned helplessness in any area of your life?
2. What fears stop you from going after your dreams?
3. What action do you need to take to establish a strong faith in yourself?
4. If you weren't afraid, what would you go for?
5. What will become possible when you establish a plan for your life and work?

Wrapping It Up

The process of manifestation is powerful. It is made even more so when you decide to conquer the factors of learned helplessness, fear, and living without a plan. Once you've taken on this triad of obstacles, you are ready to decide what you want for yourself and your life. You'll begin by establishing a vision.

VISION

A vision is a picture of the future. It's the fertile ground that provides a home for your dreams to take root. When you're able to envision the life you want, you empower yourself to move toward that ideal. As you paint a picture in your mind's eye, your dreams begin to take physical form.

Any reality you can imagine has the potential to exist. The most satisfied lives, the greatest accomplishments, and the most powerful contributions begin with a vision. As we enter the process of envisioning your ideal life, I challenge you to suspend your judgments and disbelief. Throw the idea of realism out the window.

Instead, pull yourself back to your early childhood. Do you remember the anticipation you felt as you wrote out your Christmas list? Your belief in the magic of Santa Claus allowed you to aim high. Liken the energy of manifestation to the omnipotence of Santa Claus. Shoot for the stars as you design your ideal life!

THE DEPARTMENTS OF YOUR LIFE

If you were running a business, you'd accomplish your objectives through the contribution of distinct departments. Your business would require a development department to create a product or service, a marketing department to tell people about it, a sales department to sell your offering, and a finance department to handle the exchange of money. Each of these departments would have clear responsibilities in supporting the overriding objectives of your company, and they would depend on one another's performance to succeed.

If you want to live in balance and fulfillment, the departments of your life must operate in similar fashion. Each area must have a distinct objective that contributes to your vision, well-being, and happiness, and each will depend on the others to succeed.

I use six departments in the life design work I do with clients. In my experience, crafting a vision and plan around these key categories creates a blueprint for a life of fulfillment, satisfaction, and balance.

Self-Care

How are you going to take care of yourself? This is the primary question in the department of self-care. In this area you take responsibility for managing your physical health, nutrition, rest, fitness, emotional wellness, spirituality, and beauty.

There is an old adage that teaches us that what we experience in our internal world manifests in our external world. While I believe this is true, I've also witnessed the reverse of this reality. When you are happy about the way you look and feel, you begin to see the world differently. Your response to an external shift in your appearance or an increase in your wellness can powerfully revitalize your internal world.

Some of the greatest contributors to life dissatisfaction include feeling unhappy about the way you look, feeling disconnected from your purpose, and feeling emotionally depleted. While I'm not suggesting you shoot for an *Extreme Makeover*, I am encouraging you to invest in caring for your body, emotions, and spirit.

How will you commit to taking care of yourself? Perhaps you'd like to make exercise a part of your life. Maybe establishing a sound nutrition plan would allow you to nurture your health while obtaining a weight you're happy with. Could you benefit from getting a specific amount of sleep each night? How long has it been since you've had an annual physical?

What will you do to nurture your level of self-knowledge and the connection you have with your spirit? Mind you, connecting with your spirit need not have any religious connotation, unless that works for you. Ultimately, a connection with your spirit is nothing more than a connection with your authentic self. You were born to recognize and develop your potential. Your ability to clearly know who you are, what you believe in, and what you're committed to is a direct result of the time and energy you dedicate to this vital self-connection. Take care of your authentic self, and she'll take care of you.

Relationships

The relationships you share with others infuse your life with richness and texture. Your bond with your mate, your connection with your children, your kinship with extended family, your closeness with friends, and your participation in your community are imperative components to a balanced and fulfilled existence.

What kind of intimate relationship would you like to have? If you don't have children, do you want them? If you do, what kind of influence will you be in their lives? What kind of friend do you want to be? How would you like to interact with your extended family? What would you like to give to your community? (Don't you hate it when someone peppers you with a series of questions?)

When you decide on the kind of relationships you'd like to have and the quality of connections you wish to establish, you create opportunities for these bonds to form and deepen. Ultimately, when everything else in life seems chaotic or disappointing, your relationships will lift you up. Make a choice to develop and nurture key connections in your life and your experience of love, acceptance, and enjoyment will increase exponentially!

Finance

How will you manage your financial resources? The vision you establish for your financial life governs the way you earn, manage, and spend your money. You pay your bills, make and manage investments, purchase things you want and need, and plan for the future in this department of life. It is in this area that you show yourself whether or not you are a good steward of money, thus inviting or repelling additional financial abundance and prosperity into your life.

Are you financially responsible? Do you have a plan for the use of your money? Do you know what amount you need to have invested to support you in retirement? Have you established college funds for your children if you have them? Do you pay your bills on time each month? Are you in debt, or have you established a cash reserve to support your family in the event of an emergency? Are you committed to increasing your financial knowledge?

These are important questions to ponder. Your vision and corresponding plan in this area can provide you with resources to fund all of your life's dreams, or it can undermine your hopes with feelings of lack and helplessness. Choose empowerment. No matter what your situation is today, you have the ability to create a strong reality. Your power is unleashed when you define a clear financial vision and take action to make your dream a reality.

Home

Your environment is pivotal to your sense of well-being. Your home can be your sanctuary and an expression of your personality. It can nurture and soothe you, or it can frustrate and stress you.

The combined factors of the way your home looks and the strategies you use to manage it are governed in this life department. Does your home reflect your aesthetic tastes? Are you happy with your décor, or could your surroundings use a facelift? If you were going to make some changes, what type of improvements would be ideal?

Does your home reflect the standards you're comfortable with? Have you established routines to support normal household tasks such as cleaning and stocking supplies? Do you need to address any repairs? What would make managing your home easier? What would it take for you to thoroughly enjoy your surroundings?

Career

Most of us spend more time working than we do in any other area of our lives. If this is fact for you, it seems imperative that you invest yourself in a career that satisfies you and allows you to participate in ways that make you feel proud. In *Career*, you manage your day-to-day professional responsibilities, invest in your professional growth, establish and maintain peer relationships, and envision the path you'd like to follow in your occupational development.

I'd like to take just a moment to address all of the stay-at-home mothers who might be reading this book. There is almost no statement that frustrates me more than "Oh, I'm just a mom." Just a mom? Just a mom? What does that mean? As far as I'm concerned, all of the "just mothers" out there are raising our future!

If you are a stay-at-home mom, your career department is designed to help you do your job beautifully. Ultimately, that job involves running your household and family. You are the CEO of your home! I challenge you to view this category with that perspective, rather than simply shrugging it off. If you've decided that your job involves staying at home to raise your children, then commit to doing that job beautifully. Take pride in it, and stretch yourself to do the best possible job you're capable of.

If you find yourself in the corporate or small business world, consider whether or not your current activities fulfill you. Do you feel satisfied at the end of each day? Do you enjoy most of what you're doing? What would you like to accomplish? Is there a specific level of leadership you'd like to attain or a revenue-based goal you'd like to reach? How can you stretch yourself to get stronger, more capable, more competent, and thus more satisfied?

Personal Growth and Experience

This is one of my favorite departments. It dictates what kind of encounters you want to have in your life. It literally defines the essence and texture of your overall life experience. What kind of person will you be? What kind of knowledge will you develop? What adventures will you embrace?

What parts of the world would you like to visit? Would you like to speak another language? Are you interested in mastering a specific sport or hobby? What could you do with your creative impulses? For that matter, what kind of experiences would you like to have on a regular basis? Do you enjoy going to the movies, taking in a play, or listening to a certain kind of music? What excites and satisfies you?

Every experience in your life impacts you in one way or another. When you consciously decide what kind of experiences you want to have, you begin to influence the effect that life has on who you are. In this department of your life, you take charge of your personal experience.

CALL TO ACTION – ENVISION YOUR IDEAL

It's time for you to envision your ideal life. Set aside between thirty and sixty minutes and consider what you want in each of the departments of your life. Remember to suspend realism for a moment and really connect with the desires of your heart. Don't worry about how you'll accomplish what you write down. We'll get to that shortly. For now, step into the belief system that if you can envision it you can make it happen, and answer the following questions.

1. How do you want to take care of yourself? What will you commit to in the area of Self-Care?
2. What kind of connections do you want to share with others? What will you create in the area of Relationships?
3. What would your financial ideal look like? What do you want for your Finances?
4. Imagine your ideal Home. What are you committed to developing in this area?
5. If you could develop any kind of Career, what would you want for yourself?
6. What kind of life experiences would you like to have? Describe your ideal for the category of Personal Growth and Experience.

Wrapping It Up

Congratulations! You've just completed a crucial exercise! Knowing what you want is more than half of what is required to get you there. Your willingness to consider the ideal you'd like to create in each area of your life sends a powerful message to your body, mind, and spirit—the message that it's time to stop settling. It's time to start living the life of your dreams. Now, let's take a look at how to make that happen.

MAKE IT HAPPEN

In the moment you define what you want, you engage a powerful process that orients your focus and increases your awareness of opportunities to support your dreams. This process is called sensory acuity.

Human beings can only take in a limited amount of information at any given time. In our day-to-day lives, we are bombarded with almost limitless data. In order to support us, our brains filter much of this information, allowing only those pieces of data that seem meaningful, based on our current state of mind, to factor into our awareness.

Can you remember making a decision to buy a new car, only to notice that car everywhere you drove? Can you recall deciding to take up a new hobby, only to detect information about the new activity all around you? This was not coincidence. This was simply your sensory acuity kicking into gear.

Those cars had always been on the road—you just hadn't noticed them before. There had always been information about your new hobby around you. It just hadn't registered until you let your brain know that it mattered to you. Once you sent your brain the message that you were interested, it opened the gates of your mind to recognition of what you'd decided you were curious about.

When you clearly define what you want, your brain is able to use your desires to refine the filters it will refer to when processing the information around you. As a result, you become more sensitive to both those opportunities that may have always existed in your life and any new information that could help you achieve your goals.

The more clearly you've defined what you want, the more powerfully the process of sensory acuity will support you. In fact, once you clearly map the steps you need to take to breathe life into your vision, you'll be surprised at how many resources you discover at your immediate disposal.

MAP THE GAP

When you *Map the Gap*, you define and organize the steps you'll need to take to bridge the gap between where you are today and where you'd like to be. This exercise takes the big picture of all that needs to be accomplished and establishes the individual goals and outcomes that will support your end game. Essentially, it puts your process into baby steps, which helps you focus on one manageable goal at a time instead of the seemingly overwhelming gap that exists between your present and desired circumstances.

The mapping process is very simple, and involves three basic questions: What do you want? Where are you now? What must you accomplish to create what you want?

What Do You Want?

You've already completed this process. You've consciously decided what you want in every area of your life and work. As we've discussed, this knowledge kicks your brain into high gear. You may not realize it yet, but your sensory acuity is already at work!

Your brain is the most powerful computer in the world. It is designed to support you in manifesting your aspirations. Remember to engage this powerful ally every day. Regularly check in with your dreams to remind yourself of the vision you hold for your life.

Some experts recommend writing your top goals (we'll get to those in a moment) down on paper and reviewing them each day. Others recommend reviewing them once a week. Select the process that works for you and commit to checking in with your dreams on a regular basis. This very simple process will help you keep your eye on the ball amidst even the most stressful times.

Where Are You Now?

You must define your starting point before you can begin your journey to success and fulfillment. Consider each area of your life and work. How are you doing? How far off the mark are you from the ideal you envisioned in each area?

It's important not to get frustrated when moving through this process. It's normal to be pretty far off the mark in a number of areas. Don't allow that to disappoint you. On the contrary, get excited about your discovery!

Allow me to remind you, you cannot change what you do not acknowledge, but once you acknowledge the truth of any situation you empower yourself to improve upon it. Dissatisfaction is motivating! Remember our discussion about learned helplessness? If you're not really dissatisfied with your life circumstances, you're unlikely to change them! Dissatisfaction breeds action, and action is required if you're going to reach your ideal.

What Must You Accomplish to Create What You Want?

Once you're clear about what you want and where you are, it's time to create a plan of action to move you between those two points. This is the phase in your process where you will make a list of the specific results you want to create in your life, the actions that will help you accomplish them, and the resources you can draw upon to support you.

Results – A result is an outcome that is required to support your overall vision. For example, if you decided that you'd like to build a lean, healthy, energetic body and you're carrying twenty pounds of body fat, one result you'll need to create is the elimination of the extra fat on your frame.

Actions – Your actions are the specific things you must do in order to create your desired results. Using our current example, some specific actions you might take could include committing to daily exercise and establishing an eating plan that would support your fat-loss efforts in a healthy and sustainable way.

Resources – A resource is something that can be drawn upon to help you take the actions you need to take. In the instance of committing to daily exercise, you could join your local gym and hire a personal trainer to get you started with an effective training program. You could refer to a well-respected nutrition book or invest in a consultation with a nutritionist to design a sensible eating plan. In these instances, your gym, the trainer, the nutrition book, and the nutritionist would all serve as resources that support your overriding objective to lose twenty pounds of body fat.

One Step at a Time

It's advisable to move through this process for each of your life departments. Once you've completed the initial mapping process, you'll have a fairly clear blueprint of the specific results you need to create in each area of your life. While this is very exciting, initially it can also feel overwhelming. Looking at your completed map may cause you to feel like you have an inordinate number of things to accomplish.

To avoid overwhelm, I suggest prioritizing your lists and committing to going for one result at a time. Take a look at the results you want to create and ask yourself which result must come first, which second, and so on. Once you've ordered your results, give your full attention to just one at a time in each of your life departments.

This approach helps you put a manageable framework around your activities. While you'll be making massive progress in each area of your life, your clear focus will give you a sense of emotional equilibrium and self-mastery. This is the foundation of a well-balanced life.

CALL TO ACTION – MAP THE GAP

It's time for you to create your plan of action. You'll need about one hour for this activity. You can complete it in small chunks or set aside the full hour to nail it down. While I asked you to suspend realism during your visioning process, I invite you to bring it back into play for this exercise. Make sure that you literally get real with yourself. To turn your vision into a reality, you must acknowledge where you are now and clearly define what you need to accomplish. For each of the departments of your life, reconnect with what you want by referring back to your vision and then answer the questions below.

1. Where are you now? Define your current circumstances.
2. What results do you need to create to get where you want to be?
3. Order your results. Which must you accomplish first, which second, which third, and so on?
4. Consider your first result. What actions must you take to create the outcome you're committed to?
5. What resources can you draw upon to support you?

CLIENT PROFILE – HAILEY

Hailey hired me to help her find a husband. She was a successful small-business owner in her late thirties with a bright personality and piercing green eyes. During our initial appointment, she let me know that her "biological clock was ticking" and that she needed to have a baby within the next two years. This goal-oriented woman reasoned that to accomplish her objective she needed to meet the man of her dreams within three months, marry within six, and become immediately pregnant.

Hailey was focused, clear about her intention, and matter-of-fact in her approach. While I appreciated these attributes, I was fairly certain that there was more going on with her than the natural and normal desire to start a family.

I asked Hailey to move through an evaluation exercise with me, rating her level of satisfaction in each of the key areas of her life. As I'd suspected, she felt highly satisfied with the state of her business yet disappointed and unfulfilled in every other area of her life. As is the case with many small-business owners, Hailey's work had not just taken over her life—it had become her life.

While Hailey knew that she wasn't happy, she had not stepped back to evaluate her life as a whole. Instead she had compared her situation to those of her acquaintances and employees, and had come to the conclusion that a husband and child were the missing pieces that would make her life complete. I asked Hailey if she would give me three months to work with her in creating a whole life plan, suspending her goal to find a husband during that timeframe. If at the conclusion of our first three months she was not happy with the results of the work I was suggesting, I committed to working with her for three more months at no charge to address her original objective. She agreed.

As we moved through the life design process, Hailey began to realize that she had been living in only one area of her life for so long that she had started to assume that was normal. We began establishing a vision for each of Hailey's life areas, and she moved through the process with gusto. While working on her vision for the relationships she'd like to develop and the home she'd like to create, Hailey uncovered what was really holding her back. She was afraid.

As Hailey was growing up, her father's job had required that the family relocate every twelve to eighteen months. As a result, she drew two faulty conclusions. First, she learned that there was no need to create a home out of a house. Why put down roots when she'd be packing boxes in a few short months? Most profoundly, she made the connection that relationships weren't permanent. On the contrary, she believed they were temporary.

In one of our sessions Hailey recalled a specific experience involving her first crush, a boy she'd been certain she would marry one day. She had invested her emotions in the relationship, and was deeply hurt when the young man called it quits once Hailey's family received orders to move again.

Though she didn't do it consciously, during the course of that experience Hailey linked that loving someone without reservation would lead to pain—so she didn't let herself do it again. While she made friends in each new town and had several boyfriends, she never allowed herself to emotionally invest in her personal relationships. She was always ready to leave.

She shared with me that, while growing up, her school-work had been one of the only constants in her life. She had developed and used the same process to study and complete assignments at every school she had attended. She realized that, as an adult, her work had taken the place of her studies.

Her business revolved around process and predictability, which made her feel safe and in control. It also provided her with a great excuse to avoid taking risks in other areas of her life. She was always "too busy" to make a good friend, decorate her home, or develop a solid love connection. As a result of her fear, she had settled into her own version of learned helplessness.

I'll never forget the look on Hailey's face when she made this realization. It was as if something had been turned on inside her. There was a light in her eyes as she said, "You know what, Kim? I'm a big girl now. I'm the only one who can decide it's time for me to pick up and move. I'm ready to have a full life!"

We completed her design process, and Hailey established a clear vision with supporting goals in each life area. Within eight weeks she had decorated her townhome, joined a local women's organization, started attending a yoga class, and taken up horseback riding, an activity she'd always wanted to try. She was making new friends, and while she was "busier than ever" it was with a full balance of activities that allowed her to experience her whole life rather than one small part of it.

At the end of our three months together, Hailey decided she didn't want to work toward her original goal. Instead, she thought she'd enjoy her new life for a bit. She promised to call me if she changed her mind.

As it turned out, she called me about two months later. She had met an interesting man at the stables and was excited about the prospect of dating him. We worked together for about three more months after that, as I helped Hailey increase her personal faith to the point where she could comfortably allow herself to establish an intimate connection with her new friend. About one year later, I received an invitation to Hailey's wedding.

She's not pregnant yet, but has assured me that she is happier today than she's ever been. "I'm living a full life now. I'm very busy, I'm definitely not in control, but I am in joy. When it's time to have a baby, I'll be a much better mother because I've learned how to love living!"

Hailey's story is powerful for many reasons. Her willingness to look at her whole life before zeroing in on a smaller goal allowed her to expand her view of living. Her willingness to identify her limitations and work toward strengthening her faith allowed her to overcome her fear of intimacy. Her newfound courage supported her in finding an ideal mate—and in creating a full and happy life.

Wrapping It Up

When you dare to look inside yourself and give voice to the quiet whispers of your heart, you initiate a powerful cycle that will support the birth of your wildest dreams. Yet, your dreams remain just that—dreams—until you write them down. This simple act makes them possible. Your willingness to map a plan of action makes them probable. Your commitment to acting on them each day makes them reality.

KEY LEARNING POINTS

• A balanced life is, in essence, a designed life. It is a life that has been clearly crafted, carefully nurtured, and intentionally acted upon.

• Three common obstacles to living the life of your dreams include learned helplessness, fear, and the absence of a plan.

• A vision is a picture of the future. It's the fertile ground that provides a home for your dreams to take root. When you're able to envision the life you want, you empower yourself to move toward that ideal.

• There are six key areas involved in designing a well-balanced life. They include self-care, finances, relationships, home, career, and personal experience. Each area has specific objectives that contribute to your vision, well-being, and happiness, and each depends on the others to succeed.

• The process of making your dreams come true involves staying focused on what you want, identifying where you are now, and creating a plan of action that includes results, actions, and resources.

ESTABLISH KEY CONNECTIONS: RICH RELATIONSHIPS

At this point in your process, congratulations are in order. You're well on your way to creating a life of balance, fulfillment, and abundance. Throughout this journey, I'm sure you've learned many things about yourself. Some of what you've uncovered may have surprised you. Other parts of your discovery may have sobered you. Still others likely excited you.

While the work of self-improvement is never really finished, you have started to lay the foundation that will allow you to move out into the world, continually learning, growing, and evolving, while maintaining your sense of personal balance. If you haven't already, you can expect to begin feeling comfortable in your own skin shortly. You can expect to start liking the woman you are, and to become more comfortable taking risks. Rather than allow your fear to suffocate you, you'll now begin to acknowledge and step through it.

If you're not quite there yet, never fear. It doesn't matter how rapidly your personal evolution manifests, it is already in process and you can rest assured that it will make itself known very soon. In this stage of personal transition you are ready to invite a heightened level of joy into your day-to-day experience. This joyful opportunity can be found in your relationships.

Interpersonal connections are the juice of life. The bond you have with yourself, the connection you share with your life partner, and the kinship you develop with your family and friends are the threads that weave the quilt of your life. These attachments provide a home for your emotional experience, which feeds your spirit.

In Step 5, I asked you to envision what you wanted for yourself in the area of relationships. By now you have a clear idea about the kind of connections you want to share with others, and you may have an understanding about what you'll need to do to create them. In this step, we're going to take a look at several relationships I've found to be of great importance in a woman's life and we'll consider how your ability to form, nurture, and expand relationships can enhance your life.

THE ESSENTIAL SIX RELATIONSHIPS

You will have the opportunity to participate in many relationships throughout your lifetime. In my work with clients, I've identified six primary relationship categories. Each of them addresses a unique set of needs and desires and requires a specific contribution on your part. The bonds you develop in each of these areas can support you in becoming the balanced, happy, satisfied human being you've decided to be. Let's take a look at these six affiliations.

THE SELF-CONNECTION

The relationship you develop with yourself will be the most pivotal connection you make in your lifetime. This is the link that allows you to understand what you want, who you are, and how you want to live your life. Your self-connection will ground you and give you a sense of certainty that will allow you to move past your social mask and beyond the bravado of ego. Your self is the core of who you are—it will always lead you down a path of joy and empowerment.

The intimacy you experience with your core forms the basis of every other relationship you have. When you accept yourself, you will more easily accept others. Your ability to like, support, and appreciate yourself will make you much more likely to like, support, and appreciate the people in your life.

In the next section, you will find an overview of the many strategies you can use to form and nurture this pivotal connection. For now, embrace the concept that no other relationship investment you make will be more profound or sustaining than the bond you develop with your core.

THE MATE CONNECTION

Sharing an intimate partnership with another human being is a primal requirement. Our needs for love, acceptance, support, physical contact, and intimacy are satisfied in healthy love relationships. In its highest form, the bond you share with your mate allows you to give and receive, satisfies your need to feel significant, and inspires you to explore your capabilities as you co-create a mutual reality. This mutuality supports you in feeling that you are not alone, and it motivates you to embrace the best parts of yourself.

In their lower form, love relationships can magnify our deepest fears and insecurities. For this reason, it's important to have formed a deep and sustainable link with yourself before moving into a committed partnership with a mate. Your personal connection dictates the type of individual you attract, the standards you set for the union, your capacity to communicate with your partner, and your participation in the growth and evolution of your relationship.

If you're already in a committed union, take inventory. What is it about your partnership that works? What doesn't work? What are you doing to contribute to the health of your interaction? What are you doing to detract from it? Commit to investing in your self-connection as you focus on nurturing the link you share with your mate. Envision the quality of the association you'd like to share with your partner, and define the things both of you will need to do and stop doing to make your vision a reality.

If you aren't yet in a love relationship but would like to be, decide to invest in creating a great life. Invariably, when you're looking for love, it eludes you. Conversely, when you focus on developing a high-quality self-connection and a life that fills you up, love will find you. Don't put your dreams on hold until you find that special someone. Go for them! Focus each day on creating a reality that enthralls you; then, when you do find the person of your dreams, the rest of you will be ready for him.

The opportunity to share an intimate connection with another human being can profoundly affect your life. Offering another person acceptance, support, love, friendship, and commitment will inspire your own growth, and allowing yourself to receive these same gifts will cause your heart to overflow. The magical opportunity to co-create your lives, share your triumphs and struggles, and quite possibly raise a family offers some of life's greatest rewards. Make nurturing the relationship you share with your life partner one of your top priorities and you will find yourself madly in love with your mate and head over heels in love with your life.

CLIENT PROFILE – SHARON

Sharon was a vivacious, professional woman in her early forties. She'd spent the better part of her twenties and thirties focused on her career. As a result of her keen business acumen and intense personal discipline, she had built a thriving executive recruiting company. She was financially and professionally successful, but she felt as if something was missing in her life.

Sharon began to work with me to establish personal balance. While she was proud of her professional accomplishments, she desperately wanted to get married and start a family. During one of our first sessions, I asked Sharon to describe the life she imagined as a married woman with children. She explained to me that she would have the home of her dreams, which she was able to describe in great detail. She talked about the sense of satisfaction she would get from openly sharing herself with her partner and from nurturing a young child. She talked about planning for her financial future and imagined how secure she would feel knowing that she'd completed a will and put her financial affairs in order.

As we talked, I asked Sharon why she believed she had to be married to have the home of her dreams, put her financial affairs in order, or nurture a child. She was momentarily stumped. Finally, she said she'd always bought into the traditional picture of getting married, buying a first house, raising a family, and planning for the future with a mate. It hadn't occurred to this professionally astute woman that she could satisfy many of these desires on her own. Together, Sharon and I created a plan to fulfill her personal aspirations, and we identified opportunities for her to get out into the community to meet new people. Within six months, she had purchased her dream house, had started working with a financial planner, and had become a volunteer at a local children's organization. She was having a wonderful time decorating her new home, felt satisfied and secure with the progression of her financial activities, and had fallen in love with her job as a volunteer at the children's shelter. Her desire to open herself up and nurture another human being was being fulfilled.

It was during our fifth month of work together that Sharon came bouncing into my office, bursting with enthusiasm. She'd met "the man," another volunteer at the children's shelter. Now, one year later, Sharon and her beau are engaged to be married. Once Sharon decided to stop waiting and to give herself a great life, life gave her the love she'd been searching for.

THE PARENT OR AUTHORITY-FIGURE CONNECTION

The relationships you've established with the parental or authority figures in your life form the basis for your beliefs about your own adequacy and worth. As a child, you were entirely dependent on your parents or guardians. The way they cared for you taught you how valuable you were.

If your parents were not nurturing, supportive, or encouraging, you may harbor doubts about your own worthiness. This may cause you to hold yourself back from going after what you desire most. Conversely, if you grew up with parents who spent time with you and reinforced your personal significance, you're more likely to have self-confidence and high self-esteem.

There's good news and bad news—the bad news being that you can't erase the past. If you weren't raised in a loving environment, you can't change that experience. On the brighter side, right now you can give yourself what you most needed from your parents, even if they're not capable of fulfilling your desires or are no longer living.

If your parents are alive and if you have a good relationship with them, count your blessings and nurture your bond. If your folks are not alive or you don't have a positive link, you can still give yourself the gift of the parental connection.

You do that by cultivating a relationship with an authority figure who will listen to you, validate you, support you, and give you unconditional acceptance. Many professionals can fill this role for you. A counselor, a therapist, a pastor, or a personal coach can prove to be a valuable ally.

If working with a professional does not appeal to you, consider cultivating a relationship with an older person in your family circle, such as an aunt or uncle. If you don't have access to such a relative, you can seek out the company of an older community member or establish a friendship with the resident of a senior citizen's home. The elderly have a great deal of wisdom and life experience to share with the younger generation, and most are willing to relate what they've learned.

When you give yourself the gift of establishing this powerful connection, the doubting child within you will grow stronger, more daring, and ever more confident.

THE CHILD OR DEPENDENT CONNECTION

We all need to be needed. The connection you share with a child or dependent directly addresses this need. When you feel unequivocally responsible for the well-being of a child or an animal, you will be prompted to reach new levels of maturity and selflessness. The knowledge that you're contributing to the wellness, satisfaction, and esteem of another being is both inspiring and sobering.

If you are a parent already, I encourage you to consciously define the relationship you want to have with your children. Ultimately, you are responsible for the quality of your interaction. Your approach sets the tone of the connection, and your behavior either validates and enforces or undermines and detracts from your children's beliefs about their personal value.

What do you want to teach your children about themselves? What messages would you like to impart about life? What value system would you like to demonstrate for them? Are you conducting yourself and contributing to your connection with them in ways that support your intent? What are you doing to contribute to or detract from your children's views of themselves and the world?

When you are a parent, you must take responsibility for living your life as a role model. Your children learn what they live, not what they hear. Take a hard look at how you're currently investing in these relationships and make sure your behavior serves both you and your children. Your willingness to do so will support your own growth, fulfill your need to contribute, and serve the greater needs of the children who depend on you for safety, sustenance, and love.

If you don't have children, you can address your need to provide a dependent with love and care in a number of different ways. You can volunteer at an organization that serves children. There is no shortage of young people in this world who need the attention of a caring and validating adult. Take a look around your own family or community. Perhaps there is a niece, nephew, or neighbor child you can invest your time, love, and energy in.

Alternatively, you could care for an animal. Fewer creatures are more defenseless and in need of our commitment than animals. Many organizations and shelters dedicate themselves to championing these interests. Your willingness to lend your support could fill your own need to provide love while greatly contributing to the well-being of an animal.

Whatever you decide to commit to, commit wholeheartedly. When another living being depends on you, you will rise to the occasion. Your potential will blossom, and the strongest, most powerful, most resilient part of your spirit will have a chance to soar. You'll be rewarded with a deep sense of personal satisfaction and an overflowing heart.

THE FRIEND CONNECTION

We all need affiliations with people we enjoy. Our friends are those people we elect to share our time and our lives with. We aren't born into these connections as we are with our family. We aren't required to function with these individuals, as is the case with our co-workers. Rather, we are attracted to the energy, the vitality, the characteristics, and the personalities of our friends. We choose to be with them because we enjoy them, and it's this choice that makes friendship so powerful.

These relationships allow us to give and receive. They provide us with a place to share common interests and may introduce us to new ones. They allow us to express ourselves and help us to evolve our own listening and relating skills. In their most empowering form, friendships meet our need for acceptance, allow us to feel as if we belong, and validate our deservingness for inclusion and attention.

In the fast-paced world we live in, friendships may be the most difficult relationships to cultivate and maintain. When you were in school, you found yourself among many people of similar age and life circumstances who were available to form bonds. Most likely, your only responsibilities at that time involved homework and household chores. The prevalent supply of candidates for friendship and the ample time available to form friendly connections resulted in relationships that developed quite naturally.

On the other hand, now that your life follows the unique twists and turns of adulthood, you're rarely thrown into situations where friendship candidates are in abundance. When you do meet someone you could share a connection with, you may be so overscheduled that you squelch your inclination to issue an invitation. How can you invite someone to lunch or a cup of coffee when it's a rare occasion for you to sit down to one yourself?

As you begin to align your time with your priorities throughout this program, your opportunities for establishing friendships will increase. You must then decide who you're going to be friends with.

I'm a big believer in quality over quantity. I prefer the close connection of two or three great friends to the superficial social interaction of larger groups. While the choice is certainly yours to make, I encourage you to commit the time you've set aside for friendship to those people you most admire, respect, and enjoy. Your investment will support the development of true bonds, which will allow you to experience authentic kinship and intimacy. Your ability to be truly yourself when you're with these friends will contribute to your overall capacity to let loose and enjoy yourself.

If you can envision yourself making the time, but have no idea whom you might spend it with, never fear. You're not alone. In many instances, by the time you make yourself available to invest in friendship, the people you used to share relationships with will have moved on. You can make an effort to rekindle old connections, to develop new ones, or to do some combination of the two.

To reconnect with old friends, simply pick up the telephone. Most of us lead busy lives. A true friend will not only be thrilled to hear from you, she'll understand that the many demands of life caused you to be less available than you would have liked to be. Make sure you let this person know that you miss her and that you're really committed to developing and nurturing your friendship now. Make a regular date to invest time in this bond. You may decide to get together once a week for coffee or once a month for lunch. The frequency of your meetings and the activities you engage in are unimportant. What matters is your commitment to be there for each other. Focus on that commitment and follow through with your agreements. You'll be rewarded with a flourishing friendship and many good times.

Meeting new people can be a bit more daunting. Again, we're all so busy. Many times, you will hesitate to extend an invitation simply because you don't want to impose on another person's already active life. If you keep in mind that we all benefit from the bond of friendship, you will feel emboldened to reach out when you do find yourself interested in connecting with a new person.

You can meet new people in many different places. Is there a person in your neighborhood or community you've always found interesting? Perhaps you could invite someone from your health club, your hair salon, or your children's school for a cup of coffee one morning. Can you think of anyone at the office or within an organization you belong to who might be interesting to know? Take a moment and see who comes to mind. Then, reach out, and invite her to join you for a simple cup of coffee or a walk. Everyone enjoys authentic connection. If you approach people with a genuine interest in getting to know them, it's quite likely they'll reciprocate.

Your investment in friendship invites simple enjoyment back into your life. The busy adult you are now needs to have fun, communicate, and share interests with others as much as the child you once were did. Give yourself permission to play!

CLIENT PROFILE – ALISE

A busy mother of three young children, Alise was in her late thirties and had recently moved to a new city. She initially sought our coaching partnership to help her put some order into her chaotic schedule. Once that had been accomplished, it became apparent that she missed the camaraderie of a good girlfriend.

I asked Alise to describe the kind of woman she wanted to be friends with. How old would she be? Would she also have kids? What would her interests be? How frequently would she and Alise talk on the phone, meet in person, or communicate with each other? Alise decided she'd like to form a friendship with another busy mother and that getting together for morning coffee once a week would be a fun commitment that she could fit into her schedule. We discussed what personality traits the woman might have and what kinds of conversations she and Alise might share. Once Alise was clear about the kind of woman she'd like to invest her friendship in, I asked her to think about the people she'd met since she'd arrived in the area. After a few moments, she mentioned a woman she saw at the grocery store each week, a woman who was always friendly and willing to say hello. I asked Alise if she would be willing to introduce herself and ask the woman to have a cup of coffee the next time she saw her at the store. Alise agreed. During our next session, Alise admitted that she'd seen her potential friend at the grocery store as usual but had been too uncomfortable to introduce herself. "I feel like a shy teenager!" she exclaimed. I asked her to describe the worst thing that could happen if she asked this woman

out for coffee. Once she thought about it, she realized
that her biggest fear involved the other woman saying
no. After deciding she was willing to take this risk, she
committed to approaching her potential friend the following week.

At our next meeting, a triumphant Alise announced that
she'd had coffee with her new friend and made another
date for the following week. She had really liked the
woman and enjoyed the time they spent over coffee and
casual girl-talk. Several months later, Alise told me that
she and her new friend continue to meet weekly for coffee.
They've included several other mothers in their morning
ritual now, and their group has grown to five women.
The morning meetings have become a place for them to
connect with one another, share their lives, discuss their
challenges, and offer one another support.

Because Alise was willing to express her desire for a new
friend, risk making the first move, and demonstrate her
commitment by showing up each week, she now has a
whole circle of friends.

THE HIGHER-POWER CONNECTION

The connection you cultivate with a higher power will sustain you
through both the most joyful and most difficult times of your life. Your
belief in an omnipotent force satisfies your need for certainty and validates
the fact that you're not alone. This belief does not have to be religious.
You don't have to subscribe to any specific doctrine or pay homage to
any religious figurehead. You can simply embrace the concept that there
is a knowing, benevolent power beyond you and accept that this force has
a purpose.

Developing a set of faith-based beliefs and maintaining a link with
your own version of a higher power can give you a profound sense of

clarity and certainty when you're faced with difficult decisions or circumstances. Maintaining this association will add richness, texture, and possibly even a sense of mission to your experience of each day.

Such a link can be cultivated in a multitude of ways. For some, joining a religious community and taking part in the ritual and ceremony of worship is sustaining. For others, spending time in nature allows them to engage with a benevolent energy. For still others, reading great spiritual literature or taking part in community outreach activities fills their need for a soul-nourishing connection.

Invest in the strategy and the belief system that support you in establishing convictions to guide you through life. You will be rewarded with a deeply felt satisfaction, a clear understanding of what things mean, and a profound sense of connection to all of life.

CALL TO ACTION – YOUR ESSENTIAL SIX RELATIONSHIPS

This activity will help you to evaluate your current relationships, identify those you'd like to cultivate, and commit to those you'd like to improve. Open your journal or your computer notebook, and answer the following questions.

- Self-Connection – Do you know who you are? Do you like being with yourself? Make a commitment to follow the steps outlined in the next section of this chapter, "The Fundamentals of Self-Care," and deepen the connection you have with yourself.

- Mate Connection – If you are in a committed relationship, what are you doing to contribute to the health of that connection? What are you doing to contaminate it? If you aren't in a relationship yet, what could you do to improve the quality of your life and your connection to self?

- Parent or Authority-Figure Connection – Do you share a nurturing connection with your parents? If you do, how can you deepen and strengthen that bond? If you do not, who could you establish a connection with to fill this role in your life?

- Child or Dependent Connection – If you're a parent, what are you doing to nurture your children? What are you doing that may be harming them? If you aren't a parent, who could you invest your time in to address this relationship need?
- Friendship Connection – Who is your best friend? Is there someone in your personal or professional circle you'd like to know better? How will you cultivate and nurture that relationship?
- Higher-Power Connection – Are you interested in developing a relationship with a higher power? If so, what is the most effective action you could take to establish this connection?

THE FUNDAMENTALS OF SELF-CARE

Throughout this program I've eluded to self-care a number of times. I've encouraged you to take care of yourself *at least as well* as you take care of the other people in your life, and I've encouraged you to make time to nurture your mental, physical, emotional, and spiritual well-being. I'm so passionate about the importance of this basic tenet that I'd like to invest a few more pages in discussing why it's so important for you to take care of yourself and how you might consider doing so.

What contribution will you make to your world? Who will you touch while you have this gift of life? The answers to these questions are waiting to be discovered. They live within you, and your life begins to flow once you learn to tap into them.

This flow is engaged when you recognize and embrace the power and magnificence that exists in the core of your being. If you're like most people, this core has been quiet, dormant perhaps. She won't yell and scream to be heard. She won't interrupt the frenzied activity in your life to get your attention. Rather, she quietly whispers and patiently waits for you to hear.

Your willingness to slow down, get still, and listen allows her to start communicating with you. She has answers to every question you can ask. She knows what your strengths are, and she wants to help you direct them. She understands what your weaknesses are, and she accepts you anyway. She knows, unquestionably, what you need to live a balanced, joyful, fulfilled life, and she will tell you, if only you'll listen.

She is your guardian angel, your wisest guide, your heart's song, your internal catalyst, the voice of your soul. She is you as your most authentic self, and she wants you to know that there is no one like you in the world. There never has been and there will never be another like you again. You are an original.

Your ability to successfully make and maintain a connection with the wise guide inside of you will catalyze you to tap, explore, and evolve your unique potential. You establish and nurture this connection by developing a relationship with yourself.

DATE YOURSELF

Think back to the time when you began dating your last partner or the person you share your life with. Didn't you move heaven and earth to make yourself available to this person? Didn't you find yourself fascinated by him and giddy with enthusiasm about how wonderful he was? You couldn't stop thinking about him, couldn't stop talking about him, and wanted to spend every possible moment of your spare time with him, didn't you?

Stay in your memory for another moment. As you got to know this person, didn't you forgive his idiosyncrasies—sometimes without a second thought? Instead of focusing on his shortcomings, didn't you allow yourself to be enthralled by everything about him?

Now, what if you took a similar approach to developing a deeper level of intimacy and connection with yourself? There are three steps involved in creating a high-quality relationship with yourself. The first requires you to make time for yourself. The second involves establishing a set of rules that govern how you'll interact with yourself. And the third mandates that you follow through. This means you must demonstrate to yourself how valuable you are. You do this by making appointments to connect with yourself. You further validate your worth by spending this time gently and joyfully. And you build a repository of trust each time you show up when you said you would. Your commitment to these three steps will support you in developing a healthy, intimate connection with your authentic core.

One of the biggest obstacles you'll have to overcome once you've decided to know yourself involves making time to invest in the process. Notice I said "making" time. It's quite likely that you don't have many spare moments available in your calendar. You must make this journey a priority and begin scheduling dates with yourself.

Once you start to invest that time, you will reconnect with the person you are. You'll get reacquainted with the little things that bring you joy, the big things you dream of, the fears that hold you back, and the core beliefs that fuel you.

What you do while on your dates is much less important than your willingness to show up for them. As you get started, you may want to try some of the connection strategies I suggest to my clients when they embark on their own process of self-discovery.

KEEP A JOURNAL

Writing your thoughts on paper can be a profound experience. Keeping a journal can help you discover what you're afraid of, what you're passionate about, and what you aspire to.

Buy yourself a beautiful notebook and a pen you enjoy writing with. Find twenty quiet minutes in your day and steal away to a comfortable place. Begin by writing as if you were talking with yourself or a trusted confidant. Write about how you're feeling, what's bothering or exciting you, or the day ahead of you. Or answer questions from books you've read or personal development programs you've undertaken.

Remember that your journal is for your eyes only. You aren't going to share it with anyone, so it can be messy and illegible. It's a safe place in which you can write down the things you dare not say out loud.

Be sure to keep your journal in a secure place, and enjoy the process of establishing a connection with yourself through the written word.

MEDITATE

Meditation is not about attaining a state of emptiness while sitting in the lotus position. It's about observing yourself in the present moment and clearing yourself of negative energy.

Find a block of ten quiet moments in your day and select a place where you can sit comfortably. Make sure you won't be disturbed. Turn off the ringer on your telephone and let your kids know they shouldn't disturb you for a few moments. (I promise, they will survive.)

Focus on your breath. Allow any thoughts that enter your mind to be there. Acknowledge them, but don't focus on understanding what they mean or solving any problems. Just let them be. Your goal should be to empty yourself of anxiety and worry, not to attain a state of free-floating awareness. Just clear your energy.

If you can get past the New Age feel of meditation, it can introduce enormous benefits into your life. It enhances your ability to establish and maintain focus, and the deep breathing oxygenates your entire system, infusing you with energy. Forget about the lotus position. Just sit comfortably and clear your mind.

EXERCISE

There are numerous studies documenting the physical and emotional benefits of moving your body. Exercise can be a meditation in and of itself. If you're the type of person who has a really hard time slowing down, this may be a great way for you to begin committing to time with yourself.

Commit to spending twenty to thirty minutes each day engaging in some form of physical activity. You could join a gym and work on a cardiovascular machine such as a treadmill, stair climber, or orbital trainer. You could participate in an exercise class such as step aerobics, kickboxing, or yoga. Or you could hire a personal trainer and begin a weight-training program.

The activity you choose is not important. What matters is your commitment to investing time in your health and in your connection with yourself. If you choose to work this activity into your calendar, you'll likely experience not only the benefits of getting reacquainted with yourself but also the joy of feeling healthy, fit, and strong.

WALK

Walking is a moving meditation. It allows you to slow down and notice what's going on around you while focusing on the methodical process of putting one foot in front of the other. If you usually move a million miles a minute, walking can allow you to focus on being fully present while indulging in the movement you find so vital. Walking gives you an opportunity to mull over something that may be on your mind or to simply notice the beauty and bounty of your surroundings.

Venture out into the streets of your neighborhood or on a walking trail near your home. Go to a favorite park or drive to a wooded area or to a path near the water at a beach, lake, or riverfront. Focus on the fresh smells in the air, the beauty of the horizon, and the sounds of nature surrounding you.

For many people, the act of being in nature is truly spiritual. It connects them with their higher power, helps them to establish a level of clarity in their thinking, and provides them with the benefits of outdoor athletic activity. Set some time aside this week to give a walk a try.

LISTEN TO UPLIFTING MUSIC

Music has the power to inspire our emotions. The right song can bring us to laughter or tears. Listening closely to a favorite musical score can be incredibly uplifting. Depending on your mood, you can play a powerful classical piece, allowing your mind to move in time with the music. Or you can put an upbeat dance tune on and get up and move.

You can listen to music in so many scenarios. For example, one of my most enjoyable meditative reveries involves putting a series of my favorite CDs in my car and driving. I love to lose myself in both the score and the scenery, and I'm always energized when I return home. If you'd rather not leave the comfort of your home, you could fill a bath with hot, scented water, turn on your favorite soundtrack, and indulge yourself in the pleasure of your senses.

Visit your local music store and stock up on your favorite recordings. Fill your tape or CD changer with your new selections, and let yourself relax into the rhythm of the music. Doing so may support your engagement in a new rhythm for your life.

TAKE AN AUTHENTIC OUTING

A day spent wandering boutiques, a stolen hour in a bookstore, a mid-afternoon matinee, a journal-writing session in a coffee shop, or an afternoon being pampered at the spa—these are authentic outings, and indulging in activities like these is the epitome of dating yourself.

When you commit to embarking on a special outing for yourself, by yourself, you send your core the message that you are inherently valuable. You have no purpose in mind other than sheer indulgence, and don't you deserve it?

What are your favorite authentic outings? Do you love the theater? Could you buy yourself a ticket to a new show you'd love to see? Do you appreciate art? How about making a date to take in a new exhibit at your local museum? Love clothing or decorating? How about scheduling a date to go shopping?

Indulging the little girl within you is a marvelous way to honor yourself. Select a favorite outing and make a date with yourself to go play. You may be surprised at what great company you turn out to be.

ENGAGE IN OLD HOBBIES

What did you love to do when you were a small child? Did you make scrapbooks? Did you take dance classes, or write short stories? Perhaps you played make-believe games or put on plays. The authenticity of childhood cannot be denied.

We are closest to our most passionate interests when we are children. Unfortunately, it's not uncommon for our genuine affinity to be squelched as we take on the responsibilities of adult life. You can re-engage with your own sense of passion and play when you revisit the things you used to love to do as a child.

If you enjoyed putting on plays, perhaps you could start taking in afternoon showings, read the classics, or take a drama class. If you loved to dance, you can seek out a studio in your area and brush up on your skills. If you loved to participate in team sports, join a local athletics division and start playing again.

You will be amazed at the passion resting within you, just waiting to be rediscovered and unleashed. Embrace your natural interests and allow your enthusiasm to take flight.

CULTIVATE NEW INTERESTS

Do you have a friend who spends her time in ways you envy or admire? Did you once upon a time dream about being great at something that you've now given up on? Have you ever wished that your family had supported you in the pursuit of a special talent or interest? Give yourself permission to explore that interest now.

Investigate and research the things you find intriguing. If you admire the special dinners a friend serves, consider taking a cooking course. If you've always wondered about your musical ability, learn how to play an instrument. If you're sure there's an artist living within you, sign up for a painting or writing course. Who knows where your experimentation could lead?

You don't have to embrace your new interest with any objective in mind other than discovery. I've seen so many people embark on a new path only to push themselves to "be the best" at their undertaking. Your commitment to take piano lessons does not mean you have to become a Mozart. Joining a tennis league does not require you to be the next Chris Everett Lloyd. Instead, decide you will simply have fun with your process.

Enjoy yourself as you experiment with the many new activities that can support you in learning about yourself. If you undertake something that turns out to be less fun than you thought it would be, give yourself permission to stop. Conversely, if you discover a new hobby you love, consider integrating it into your life. Above all, have fun, and continually explore.

ESTABLISH YOUR RULES OF ENGAGEMENT

It's quite possible you've developed a tendency to be hard on yourself. In my work with clients, I've been consistently amazed at the ferocious and destructive quality of their self-talk. If your authentic self is going to venture forth, she has to know she's stepping into safe territory. You'll make this possible when you establish a set of rules to govern your self-interaction.

FORGIVE YOUR IMPERFECTIONS

The quest for perfection will lead you to frustration, exhaustion, and failure. This is because perfection, in and of itself, is unattainable, and the more valiantly you strive to reach it the farther you will fall from it.

You are a human being. Your very nature is imperfect. Your life has been set up to offer you opportunities for learning, growth, contribution, and personal evolution. These opportunities would not be necessary if you had already mastered all aspects of life.

Rather than strive for perfection, commit to excellence. Accept who you are, embrace the life experience you've had, and reconcile yourself to both your strengths and weaknesses. Decide to make small improvements in your life and your person each day, and take satisfaction in your process of growth and mastery.

BE UNCONDITIONALLY CONSTRUCTIVE

Speak kindly to yourself. You need to be the safest, most validating and supportive force in your life. Certainly, acknowledge a mistake when you make one. Be real about what's working in your life and what's not. Be honest with yourself about the behaviors you need to change and the new skills you need to learn. But do so with a spirit of kindness and grace.

Your internal dialogue, the way you speak to yourself, should be positive, affirming, and uplifting—even when you're acknowledging a mistake you've made. Be clear with yourself about what needs to change, but don't beat yourself up about the fact that you need to improve. We all do.

Your mother probably taught you to treat others as you'd like to be treated. I'll challenge you to go one step further and treat yourself that way first.

BE UNCONDITIONALLY CONSTRUCTIVE

If You Usually Say This . . .	Try This Instead . . .
I don't know the answer.	I can find the answer.
I don't know how to do that.	I may not know how to do this now, but I can learn to do anything.
I never finish anything.	I may not have finished things in the past, but I'm not living in the past. I'm living in the present, and I'm committed to finishing what I start.
I can't do that.	I can do anything I set my mind to.
What if I fail?	The only way I can fail is to not try.
What if it doesn't work?	What's the worst thing that could happen? Am I willing to take that risk?
There's no way to do that.	When I'm committed, there is always a way.
I'm too young.	I have so much youthful energy to draw upon.

If You Usually Say This . . .	Try This Instead . . .
I'm too old.	I have so much wisdom and life experience under my belt.
Nothing ever works out for me.	I can make any situation work for myself.
Bad things always happen to me.	I am not a victim, and everything happens for a reason. I am capable of dealing with anything that comes my way.
I don't follow through on commitments.	I keep my word to myself and others.
I'm not smart enough.	I am smart and capable, and I can learn to do anything.
I don't know what to do.	I trust myself to make good choices.
I don't have the right background or education.	I can combine my life experience with new training to support me in the pursuit of any goal.
The project is too big.	I will break the project down, and take one step at a time.

BE YOUR OWN BIGGEST CHEERLEADER

Everyone needs a strong support system. We all require a little encouragement when we hit a bump in the road. Each of us craves a companion to embolden us as we pursue our dreams. Be that person in your own life.

Your ability to believe, unequivocally, in your own competence will fill you with the confidence required to take risks and the sustenance needed to reach for the brass ring of life. Give yourself this gift by being the most enthusiastic, nurturing, supportive person in your life. You will be amazed at the energy and excitement you'll unleash within yourself.

GIVE CREDIT WHERE CREDIT IS DUE

Many times, we're so focused on the details of life that we forget to recognize ourselves for our accomplishments. As a result, we take very little pleasure in our achievements. We work to complete our objectives only to check off each item on our list, quickly moving on to the next goal or task. It's rare that we celebrate the accomplishment of one task before moving on to the next.

What would it take for you to give yourself a little pat on the back for your achievements each day? Is it possible to give yourself a mental high five before you go to bed at night, quietly acknowledging the tasks you completed, the quality of interaction you shared, or the difficult situation you overcame?

When you commit to recognizing yourself for your accomplishments, you'll find that you also get very good at recognizing others. Decide to give yourself this additional jolt of encouragement and acknowledgement. Your confidence will increase, and you'll look forward to congratulating yourself each day.

CLIENT PROFILE – DENISE

I began working with Denise in the early part of the year. She hired me to support her with her commitment to stick to a weight-loss program. During our first session, she explained to me that she didn't know if she would ever develop the physique she truly wanted, that she'd lost and regained the same twenty pounds time and time again, and that she lacked discipline and willpower. She told me that she couldn't seem to stick with anything for long, and she let me know how frustrated she was with herself. We worked together to establish an exercise and nutritional program to support her weight-loss goals. We also began to work on her rules of engagement.

I asked Denise to write down every negative thing she said to herself for one week and to bring her notebook to our next session. She was amazed to discover that her negative self-talk took up fourteen pages—more than two pages of destructive commentary each day.

We identified the three things she said to herself most consistently and changed them to more affirming statements. We wrote the new statements on 3 x 5 index cards, and I asked Denise to keep the cards with her at all times. Each time she began to talk negatively to herself, she was to stop mid-sentence and replace her words with one of the positive statements.

Denise participated in the process, though she was a bit dubious about carrying index cards around with her. I assured her that she would only need the cards for a week or two, just until she became conditioned to using her new statements. She agreed to give the activity a try. I also challenged Denise to consider striving for excellence rather than perfection—with her body and her life. I asked her to envision herself at her personal best rather than like a photo in a magazine, which was the ideal she'd been comparing herself to. She agreed to consider this shift in perspective. Finally, I encouraged Denise to begin recognizing her accomplishments each day by logging five achievements in her journal at night before she went to bed. Within three weeks, Denise was back in my office, looking like a new woman. She was relaxed, confident, and had lost twelve pounds. She was well on her way to her goal weight, and she was almost jumping out of her skin with enthusiasm. She said she was amazed at how powerful these simple little exercises had been. She'd never realized how much she'd undermined her own self-esteem. "I was my own worst enemy," she said. "Now, I'm my own best friend."

Denise was willing to take a look at the seemingly small things she was doing that were holding her back in a big way. She began to focus on being her personal best rather than reaching some mythical version of perfection. She turned the little voice inside her head into a cheerleader rather than a detractor, and she began to recognize herself for small successes each day. She embraced several new ideas and made a real effort to apply them to her life. As a result, Denise is living at her goal weight and feeling great about herself.

CALL TO ACTION – COMMIT TO DEEPENING YOUR PERSONAL INTIMACY

It's time for you to develop a high-quality relationship with yourself. In this exercise, I challenge you to schedule at least one date with yourself each week for the next eight weeks. For each appointment, try one of the connection strategies I've outlined for you or attempt one of your own design. Take out your calendar now and schedule your weekly date.

As you grow accustomed to showing up for yourself, pay attention to the activities that give you a true sense of satisfaction and joy. Consider integrating these activities into your routine. Let go of those that don't prove to be beneficial, and remember to observe your rules of engagement.

THE SEVEN PRINCIPLES OF RELATING

Your ability to relate measures your capacity to establish connection, rapport, and intimacy with another human being. Throughout my work as a coach, I've studied people who are masters at relating. These people have developed deep, meaningful relationships that they've sustained over long periods of time. Using those relationships as a model, I've created seven principles of relating. These are life-tested principles. When you use them, you will experience a more significant closeness with the people in your life.

BE WILLING TO RISK

Nothing great is ever accomplished without some element of risk. When you risk in relationship, you allow yourself to be vulnerable and you express your true feelings. You act in a manner that is real and honest, and you express your desire to be close to someone. You take the first step, and you act from hope instead of fear.

I'm not suggesting that you lay yourself on the line with every person you encounter. I am suggesting that when you connect with someone who meets the standards you've set for the people you want in your life, you allow yourself to take a chance.

Get clear about what you want, communicate honestly about what that is, and invest in developing the relationship rather than in protecting yourself.

It's possible that when you take this approach, you'll be hurt or disappointed. You must trust yourself enough to know that you'll select good people to let into your life and that you can handle it if someone disappoints you. The bottom line is that if you want the experience of being fully loved, you must be willing to experience full vulnerability. Be willing to take that risk.

CLIENT PROFILE – ELAINE

Elaine was a vivacious, dynamic, beautiful woman in her late twenties. She came to me for support through a career transition and to put her finances in order. During our coaching relationship, she discovered that she was falling in love with a close male friend. She wanted to pursue a more romantic relationship with him but wasn't sure how to tell him what she was feeling. In her early twenties, she'd been in a bad marriage that ended in a bitter divorce. As a result, she was dealing with a lot of past anger, and she was afraid of opening up to hurt again.

The first thing Elaine and I focused on was her experience during her first marriage. I asked her to tell me about what she'd learned in the relationship, how she had contributed to its failure, and what she needed to do to let go of her anger. Then, I asked her to describe the type of relationship she'd like to have, the kind of man she wanted to be involved with, and the kind of partner she was committed to being. We invested several weeks in this work. Finally, Elaine was ready to move to the next level. If she were going to have a chance to develop a romantic relationship with her friend, she would need to tell him how she felt, openly and honestly. She was incredibly nervous and wasn't sure she was willing to take the leap. Together, we weighed the risks. In a worst-case scenario, she could tell her friend how she felt, making him so uncomfortable that their friendship would end. Then, she wouldn't have him in her life. Or she could keep quiet, not sharing her feelings with him, and never know what kind of romantic relationship might have been possible between them. She would have him in her life, but not in the way she wanted.

Ultimately, Elaine decided she'd rather risk the friendship than be dishonest about her feelings, and she committed to telling him the truth. Her friend was surprised by her admission but was open to exploring their potential as a couple. They began dating. After several months, they decided they were better off as friends. Though they didn't end up "happily ever after," Elaine maintains that this was one of the most important romantic relationships she ever experienced. "I needed to prove to myself that I could make good choices in men, and I needed to learn to risk again. This relationship allowed me to do both of those things," she told me in a session immediately following their transition back to friendship. Almost one year later, Elaine and her friend are both dating other people—and still nurturing their friendship.

BE AVAILABLE

True intimacy can only develop over time. Relationships grow as individuals learn about each other, share secrets and dreams, and develop comfortable patterns of interaction. This evolution requires your active participation. To develop a bond, you must consistently spend time with the person you're committing to, whether in friendship or in love, and you must be present mentally and emotionally when you're together.

Be selective about the number of people you commit to in relationship. Quality by far outweighs quantity in this area of life. You will be more profoundly affected by the intimate connection to one friend than you will be by the superficial interaction with many. Once you've decided you're committed to a relationship, make it a priority. Demonstrate how much the person matters to you by showing up fully and consistently. Be available.

BE INTERESTED, NOT JUST INTERESTING

Our society is filled with people posturing for approval, working to prove their worth, and vying for acceptance. At times, even the most outwardly successful and confident spend more time talking about how interesting they are than they do finding out about the person they're talking with. This habit is nothing but a call for acceptance, approval, and belonging.

As you grow personally, you will become more confident about how worthy you are. You will understand that you are deserving of acceptance, and you will feel less of a need to prove your importance. As this shift—which is usually quite gradual—takes place, begin to focus on how interesting others are.

People really are fascinating. I've never encountered someone who didn't possess unique and special qualities, whether it was a passionate interest, a wonderful skill, a creative hobby, or a secret dream. Make the effort to learn about the people in your life. You will become interesting as a result of being interested in who others are.

BE WHO YOU ARE

Be yourself. Be honest. Don't ever pretend to be someone you aren't. Relationships require a great investment of time, intellect, and emotional currency. If you're developing a relationship based on a false self, you're doing yourself and the other person a grave disservice.

Have confidence in the magnificence of who you are. Believe in the fact that the people you want to have intimate connections with will be attracted to the real you. Not everyone will be attracted to you, but the people who are best suited to you will be.

Be honest about what you think, what you believe, and what you feel. Stay centered in the person you know you are, and remain true to your values and priorities. The people in your life who deserve your commitment will love, support, and embrace all of who you really are. Those who won't can move on—to make room in your life for those who will. Be true to yourself, be fully yourself, and accept the love you receive as a result of your authenticity.

DON'T MAKE ASSUMPTIONS

When you assume, you make something true without any proof to support your expectation. In relationship, our assumptions are usually based on our fears. We assume the worst because we fear the worst. This puts us into survival mode, which causes us to react. This cycle is at the root of many a disagreement.

When in doubt, ask. Relationship is based on communication. Your ability to clearly share, request, and exchange information will be one of the most pivotal and profound skills you'll bring to your connection.

It's okay to have doubts. It's normal to experience varying levels of fear as you move into deeper levels of intimacy with another human being. Honestly share that process with the person you're bonding with and you will watch your relationship flourish. Making assumptions contaminates relationships. Don't do it.

ACCEPT WITHOUT CONDITION

There is no such thing as a perfect human being. Every one of us has bad habits, flawed character traits, and wounds we need to heal. Don't enter into relationships with people who have flaws you cannot embrace. When you do enter a relationship, accept the other person completely.

When you fully accept others, you validate the fullness of who they are. This is incredibly empowering. When you let others know that you like, accept, and embrace them exactly as they are, you give them a true gift. This skill will allow you to form real connections because your ability to accept will make it safe for others to be themselves. From this place, you will form an honest intimacy.

This type of intimacy withstands not just the tremors of life but the earthquakes of life. Accept without condition, and you will experience real love.

GIVE WHAT YOU WANT TO RECEIVE

I'm sure your mother told you to treat others as you would like to be treated. (I know mine did!) This last principle is similar to that early life lesson. The law of reciprocity states that we will get what we put out into the world.

People respond to our expectations of them. If you're constantly focused on what you're not getting in a relationship, it's likely you're going to get even less of that. Instead, begin to focus on what you want and make the first move to add that quality or emotion to the relationship. Don't wait for the other party to do so.

If you feel a shortage of kindness, be kind. If you want to be understood, seek to understand. If you want to feel appreciated, find something to express appreciation for. If you want to be thanked, find something to thank your friend or partner for.

Be willing to make the first move, to give what you most want to receive. You will still get what you wanted, and you will get it a thousand times over.

CALL TO ACTION – APPLY THE SEVEN PRINCIPLES TO YOUR LIFE

Please get out your journal or open your computer file. In this exercise, I invite you to evaluate how well you currently use each of the seven principles in your relationships. For each one, answer the following questions.

• How well do you apply this principle to your relationships with others?

• How well do you apply this principle to the relationship you have with yourself?

• What could you do to begin strengthening your ability to apply this principle to the relationships you have with yourself and others?

Wrapping It Up

Ultimately, your ability to develop and nurture strong bonds with others will allow you to enjoy true intimacy. When you integrate these seven principles into your approach to relating, your existing relationships will become more satisfying and your ability to forge new connections will improve.

At the end of your life the memories you will cherish will be related to the connections you shared with other people. Invest in establishing, embracing, and deepening your relationships, and enjoy the magic of sharing your experience with others.

KEY LEARNING POINTS

• Investing in the *Essential Six Relationships* will help you meet your interpersonal needs while experiencing the joy and satisfaction of intimate connections.

• The relationship you develop with yourself is the most pivotal connection you'll establish in your life. It forms the basis of every other relationship you'll ever have.

• To develop a self-connection, schedule time to spend with yourself, show up for your planned appointments, and treat yourself kindly, using the *Rules of Engagement*.

• You can enhance the quality of your connections with others by observing the *Seven Principles of Relating*.

STEP 7

STAY YOUR COURSE: THE TENETS OF PERSONAL EFFECTIVENESS

Andrea was one of the most effective women I'd ever met. She was a go-getter, always developing several worthwhile projects at a time and using her laser-like focus to make things happen. She was financially successful, having made her first million by the time she was thirty years old. An optimist at heart, she had an uncanny knack for identifying the opportunity amidst even the most challenging problem. She had an engaging smile and an easy manner that allowed her to create and nurture solid connections with the people in her life, including her husband and three children. When Andrea walked into a room, you could literally feel her uplifting energy. I was fascinated by her, as was most everyone else she came in contact with.

Have you ever known an Andrea? Perhaps a colleague at your office who always seems to be on top of things, or the leader of your local non-profit organization who manages the responsibilities of her volunteer commitment and caring for her family with aplomb. Have you ever wondered what her secret is? What is it about the most effective and influential members of our society that makes them so? Have you questioned why some people seem to have it all together while others seem scattered and disjointed?

While it can sometimes seem that a chosen few have been anointed with the secrets of success, I've come to learn that there are no secrets.

Rather, there are simple principles of personal effectiveness that have stood the test of time. I've seen these principles adopted and embraced by the most fulfilled, successful people in our culture, and I've used them in my work with countless clients. It's time for you to learn about these principles and consider incorporating them into your approach to a well-balanced life.

EMBRACE PERSONAL RESPONSIBILITY

No one is responsible for your life circumstances except you. Yes, people and events may impact you in ways you cannot control, but ultimately you are the only person who can decide what you do with the experiences you've had, the dreams you aspire to, and the actions you take each day.

To be responsible quite literally means that you are "able to respond" to the events of your life. This ability to take in the present conditions of your life at any given time and to decide if those circumstances are working for you or not is always present. You always retain the power to take action and to change circumstances that aren't measuring up to your standards.

One of the most debilitating, yet common, challenges I work with clients to overcome is what I refer to as a victim mentality. Perhaps you've had a difficult childhood and that has anchored you in a self-defeating cycle of feeling powerless and devalued. It's possible that your heart was broken by an ex-lover who betrayed you or by a malicious co-worker who contributed to your being fired. In fact, it's probable that you've been on the short end of the stick at least once in your life.

Don't let these isolated experiences take away your power! It's time to get real and to think logically for a moment. Most of us had difficult childhood experiences. In fact, I've never met an individual who came from a stereotypically "functional" family. I'm not sure there is any such thing. Yet this experience doesn't keep effective people stuck in the past.

Most of us have had our hearts broken or been on the receiving end of less than optimal treatment in the workplace. Yet, the great majority of us have survived. In fact, you have too! Don't allow your victim story to rob you of the life you deserve to live. Whatever your story is, *let it go*.

Effective people don't live in the past. They've learned from the past. Then they've let it go. They live each day in the present, with their eye on the future they wish to create. When something bad happens, they take in the facts, invest themselves in their power, and take responsibility to address the situation in a way that compliments the life they want to live.

You are so powerful! Don't give your power to the past—to people who have hurt you or to the experiences that undermined your self-confidence. Step into the full magnificence of who you are, investing yourself in the belief that you can handle anything that comes your way. Then take responsibility to handle it.

CALL TO ACTION - EMBRACE YOUR RESPONSIBILITY

Answer the questions below to make sure that you're applying this principle in your life.

1. Are you allowing yourself to fall into the trap of victim mentality in any area of your life?
2. If you were assuming full responsibility for every area of your life, what action would you take?
3. Are there any areas of your life where you typically surrender your responsibility?

Based on what you've discovered, what changes could you make in your current approach to personal responsibility?

ADJUST TO CHANGE

One thing is certain in life—everything must change. Nothing is static. In fact, right now every area of your life is evolving. This truth really puts some people in a tailspin, and there is good reason for that.

We've discussed that one of your basic human needs involves your feelings of security. You must feel physically, mentally, and emotionally safe in order to live at your highest potential. One of the most common strategies used to create this sense of safety involves establishing a level of predictability in your day-to-day experience. The very nature of change shakes this predictability up.

Effective people accept the inevitability of change and consciously decide how they will embrace and manage it when it arrives. The key to successfully taking this approach requires you to identify the essence of what you value in your current circumstances and to incorporate those qualities into the changing conditions you're dealing with.

Essence is the essential quality within a specific action or experience. Within every circumstance of your life—those you love and those you don't—there is a kernel nature that impacts your perception of that event. When you experience change, it is normal for you to react to the possibility of losing that essence. Most of the time, reactions of this nature are based on fear and angst.

When you allow yourself to take a time-out and analyze the basic nature of the circumstance in your life that's changing, you are better equipped to incorporate this essence into your new circumstance.

CLIENT PROFILE – ERIN

Erin was in her late forties. She sought out my services because she was feeling depressed and isolated. She had just sent the younger of her two children off to college, and she was feeling her empty nest in an intense way. She had worked in a flower shop for more than fifteen years, usually when her kids were at school. Several months earlier the florist had shut their doors, leaving Erin without the job she'd enjoyed for as long as she could remember. To make matters worse, her husband had broached the topic of selling their family home and moving to a smaller place now that their house wasn't full of kids. Everything Erin had invested herself in was changing. She felt sad, disappointed, afraid, and very unsafe.

In our first few sessions, Erin and I explored the strategies she'd used to feel safe in the past. I learned that one of her anchors had been the quiet time she'd invested in arranging flowers each day. She talked about appreciating the beauty of the flowers and feeling close to nature as she moved through her process. We also discovered that she felt needed when her daughter had been home. She'd been very involved in the school, taking on many volunteer projects and actively participating in the PTA. She had taken pride in the contribution she'd made, and she enjoyed the feeling that her daughter needed her. She confided in me that she felt like all of those outlets had disappeared seemingly overnight. She felt disoriented, unsure about her personal value, and completely lost as to her next step. I suggested we work together to create some alternative activities Erin could experiment with. While she'd loved her job at the florist, its value had not been related to her income. She lived a very comfortable life and wasn't concerned with duplicating her salary. For this reason, I suggested Erin do a bit of research about non-profit organizations in her area that might allow her to combine her love of flowers and nature with her desire to make a tangible contribution. She seemed dubious, but promised to move through her homework activities.

Two weeks later, Erin discovered a local agency committed to turning vacant lots in low-income neighborhoods into parks. They were more than happy to have her support.

We decided she would give the organization a test run, and she committed to one project. The test run proved to be a phenomenal success. Erin loved her work with the organization. In our last session, she shared with me that not only was she able to "get her hands in the flowers and dirt," but she also felt needed and valued by her peers at the organization.

Allowing herself to identify the essence of what she was missing and seeking ways to address those needs in her changing world allowed Erin to establish a new way of meeting her needs. Today, she is actively involved in her organization and has happily agreed to build a new and smaller home for the next phase of her life with her husband.

When the winds of change begin blowing in your life, make time to connect with the essence of the circumstances that are evolving and make plans to infuse your new conditions with those core characteristics.

CALL TO ACTION – ANALYZE YOUR CHANGE PERSONALITY

Answer the questions below to make sure that your approach to change is serving you.

1. What is your typical response to change?

2. Think about something in your life that is in the midst of change or that will change very soon. What is the essence of the circumstances that have changed or are about to be modified? How does that essence serve you?

3. What could you do to incorporate this essence in a way that serves you in the new situation you're dealing with?

Based on what you've discovered, what actions must you take to successfully adjust to change?

STAY FOCUSED

The quality of your life is directly related to what you focus on in any given moment. Focus directs your attention and clarifies your actions. Effective people are masters at establishing and maintaining focus. They focus on their dreams and the results they want to create. When they encounter a problem, they focus on solving that problem so that they can get back to moving toward their goals.

I've repeatedly seen two common mistakes made in the area of focus. Either someone has a difficult time establishing focus, or he or she isn't able to successfully maintain it once they hit a bump in the road.

Establishing focus requires that you get clear about what you want and what you have to do to get there. (You did this in Step 5, so you've got this one covered.) It also mandates that you clearly define your priorities and manage your time and energy in accordance with them. While I've seen many people successfully develop their priorities (as you did in Step 2), I've worked with far fewer who were able to manage their calendars based on that list.

Effective people are willing to say *no*. When they make a commitment, they follow through on that commitment unless they're presented with a true emergency, and before making a commitment they carefully evaluate whether or not that promise will support or detract from their present undertakings.

Now that you know what to do, it's vital that you *do what you know*. This requires self-discipline and a healthy dose of personal responsibility. Being that you're almost to the conclusion of this program, I'm confident you have both of those factors covered in spades. Use them to your advantage, and establish your focus!

Once focus is established and you begin to move toward your goals, you can be certain that you will run into obstacles. I wish that I could wave a magic wand and pronounce all barriers to accomplishment be removed from your path, but I can't. You are guaranteed to bump up against at least a few boulders as you embark on your journey. The manner in which you handle them will directly contribute to your success or failure.

I've seen this scenario one too many times. Ms. Go-Getter is going for the goal. She's created a lot of momentum and is feeling great. Then, the worst happens—she runs into an unforeseen problem. Rather than maintain focus on her original goal, Ms. Go-Getter shifts all of her energy to the problem in front of her. She invests her emotions in it, allowing herself to be frustrated by its very presence. She looks to identify the people who caused the problem, so that she can let them know she's angry. She discusses the unfairness of the problem with anyone who will listen. She has shifted her focus from her goal and is investing all of her energy in the problem. She will develop quite a relationship with this problem—albeit an unhealthy one—because the approach she's using assures it will be around for a long time to come.

Don't fall into this trap! You will have problems. You will meet obstacles. Few of your projects will go according to plan. No matter what circumstances you encounter, maintain a laser-like focus on your original goal and invest all of your energy in getting over, around, under, or through the problem you're facing. Using this approach, your problems will be short-lived and you'll reduce your frustration level exponentially.

CALL TO ACTION – STAY FOCUSED

Answer the questions below to strengthen your ability to stay focused.

1. How do you normally respond to problems?
2. Think about the results you're committed to right now, and identify any obstacles currently in your path.
3. Are you investing your energy in solving the problem, maintaining focus on the results you're looking to create, or are you focused on the problem in an unproductive way?

Based on what you've discovered, do you need to adjust your approach to the current obstacles in your path?

SURROUND YOURSELF
WITH EMPOWERING PEOPLE

Nothing will sabotage your efforts to live a healthy, balanced, fulfilled life more conclusively than surrounding yourself with people who don't support your desire to live in this manner. The most difficult course you'll chart as you make life improvements will be that of nurturing and evolving relationships with those who sustain you and identifying and terminating relationships with those who aren't willing to support your growth.

Your relationships have the capacity to lift you up. They also have the capacity to keep you stuck or tear you down. Surrounding yourself with people who support your growth is an incredibly powerful way to create a lifestyle that pulls you toward your highest potential. Surrounding yourself with people who don't will almost certainly undermine the very change that you're attempting to make.

CLIENT PROFILE – KELLY

Kelly was an energetic, exuberant young woman in her early thirties. She'd sought my counsel to help her develop a healthy lifestyle. She was thirty pounds overweight and hadn't exercised in over ten years. She was aware that she made poor food choices and that she ate for many reasons other than hunger.

Kelly and I established a plan to support her weight-loss goals. We committed to making lifestyle changes and to avoiding quick-fix solutions. She joined a gym. She hired a trainer for a single session. The trainer customized a program for her and taught her how to perform each exercise correctly. She hired a nutritionist for a one-time consultation to create a plan that included how to approach food, how many calories to consume, and the types of foods she should eat. Together, we identified the situations that might threaten Kelly's ability to follow through with her commitment to exercising or her desire to eat more healthfully, and we decided how she would handle those situations when they arose. She was on her way.

Over the course of our first three months together, Kelly's results were impressive. She'd lost twenty-two pounds, with eight more to go. She'd purchased some new clothes and invested in a new haircut. She was feeling an increase in her self-confidence and was proud of what she'd accomplished. In our fourth month, Kelly's progress stalled. She gained back two pounds and didn't seem to be enjoying her new routine as much as she initially had. When I asked her what might be at the root of her situation, she shared that she was getting a great deal of negative feedback from two important people in her life—her boyfriend and her mother.

It turned out that Kelly's mother had struggled with her weight for most of her life. She was dealing with obesity and adult-onset diabetes and was having a difficult time supporting or appreciating Kelly's progress. Kelly's boyfriend, whom she'd been dating for a little over one year, was worried that Kelly might leave him if she got, in his words, "too hot," and he was jealous of the time she spent at the gym. Both Kelly's mom and boyfriend expressed their displeasure with the changes she'd been making, and her boyfriend even let her know that he had liked her better when she was heavier.

I asked Kelly what kind of support she'd like from these two important people, and we clearly defined a standard of interaction for each relationship. Next, I asked Kelly to think about what both her mother and boyfriend might be thinking and feeling, so that she could understand where they were coming from. Then, we decided that Kelly would have a discussion with her mom and boyfriend individually, letting each know how much she valued him or her and asking for his or her support.

As it turns out, Kelly's mother hadn't realized that her influence had been so negative. She admitted that watching Kelly lose weight had made her feel even worse about her own physical predicament. She agreed to begin working with Kelly to develop a more supportive way of interacting. By the time Kelly and I concluded our work together, not only had Kelly lost those last few pounds, but her mother had also joined her at the gym and was well on her way to creating her own fit body and fit life.

Kelly's conversation with her boyfriend didn't go as well. He was angered by her requests for support and let her know that he wasn't going to change his mind about her new routine. He wasn't in favor of it and demanded that she make a choice between him and her new lifestyle. Let's just say that Kelly is still enjoying her new lifestyle.

By clearly defining the kind of support she wanted from the important people in her life, Kelly was able to make specific requests. The person who truly loved her was able to accommodate her wishes, and she was able to let go of the person who wouldn't.

Today, Kelly is in a healthy relationship with an athletic man she met at her gym. She has established a circle of friends who share her healthy interests, and working out with her mom has brought them closer together.

Your commitment to surrounding yourself with supportive people and clearly asking for the kind of support you need sets you up for success. Your willingness to develop relationships with people who share your values and interests increases your chances of success still further. Your resolve to end relationships with people who won't support or who undermine your attempts at change ensures your success, increases your satisfaction, and validates your deservingness.

Take a moment to consider the key people in your life. Are they supportive of the new things you're learning? Will they encourage you in your desire to change your behavior? Better still, will they partner with you? Don't settle for less than you deserve. Adopt the strategy of surrounding yourself with empowering people and you will step more fully into your power.

CALL TO ACTION – TAKE A PEOPLE INVENTORY

Answer the questions below to determine where you may need to request an increase in support.

1. Are the most important people in your life supportive of the changes you're making?
2. If they are, thank them!
3. If they aren't, write down the specific ways you'd like them to support you, and set aside some uninterrupted time to request their help.
4. Be prepared to walk away from relationships with people who aren't truly supporting you.

Based on your answers, do you need to make any changes in your current relationships?

MAKE YOUR HABITS WORK FOR YOU

How many times have you left home on a weekend, lost yourself in thought for just a moment, and found yourself driving the familiar route to your office or your child's school? In this moment, you fell into a well-established pattern of behavior. You weren't thinking about what you were doing. You were on autopilot and were acting out a behavior that you'd conditioned by repeating it many times.

How many times have you decided you were going to make a change? Perhaps you were going to start a new activity, such as an exercise class, or maybe you'd decided to stop indulging a bad habit, such as eating too many sweets. You jumped into your resolution with gusto, only to find yourself skipping the gym and inhaling a bag of cookies a short time later. What happened?

You were hijacked by your habits. We talked a bit about habits in Step 2. In that portion of our program, I provided you with several productive habits to consider incorporating into your life. In this step, I'd like to personalize that process.

Your habits are patterns of behavior. They've been conditioned through sheer repetition, and I'm willing to bet that most of them were conditioned without a great deal of thought or planning.

This truth would be incredibly powerful if all of your habits were empowering, but I'm fairly certain they aren't. In fact, I'll bet you've got one or two habits that undermine the very results you've committed to creating in your life.

Ultimately, your habits either serve you or they don't. When a habit serves you, it moves you closer to your vision. When it doesn't, it moves you farther away from what you want. Your willingness to examine and upgrade your habits will move you closer to living your dream.

Effective people consciously design and condition habits that bring them closer to the life they want to live. They also identify habits that could derail their progress and thoughtfully replace those patterns with more empowering alternatives.

Increase your personal effectiveness by designing and conditioning productive habits that take you closer to the life you want to live!

CALL TO ACTION – UPGRADE YOUR HABITS

Answer the questions below to identify where your habits might need to be upgraded.

1. Revisit the vision, results, and actions you established in Step 5.
2. Are your current habits moving you closer to the life you want to live? If so, which of your habits are really serving you? If not, which could change?
3. Design more empowering habits to take the place of those that aren't serving you.

Commit to conditioning your new habits! A short period of consistency will go a long way toward establishing the automated patterns that support your dreams!

Wrapping It Up

You've come a long way throughout this journey. You've learned how to manage your energy, and you've established priorities. You've connected with the emotional drivers that shape your behavior, given voice to your unique strengths, and started to learn about the values that impact your passion and purpose. You have clearly defined what you want in your life and your work, and you've created a plan to focus your daily actions. You've considered what kind of relationships you'd like to develop, and you've started to nurture your self-connection.

As a result of your thoughtful self-inquiry, you are well on your way to living a life of balance and fulfillment. You know what to do. *Now you must do what you know.*

The tenets of personal effectiveness will help you do just that. These time-tested principles have worked for many of the happiest, most respected, most successful people in our society, and they will work for you too.

Nothing is beyond you at this point. The life of your dreams is not only within your reach, it's unfolding—even in this very moment. Thank you for allowing me to be part of your journey. Continue to invest in your self-discovery, and remember to take care of yourself *at least as well* as you take care of everyone else in your life!

KEY LEARNING POINTS

- There are no secrets to success, but there are several simple principles of personal effectiveness that have stood the test of time.
- Effective people take responsibility for their lives. This means that they constantly assess their present conditions, measure them against their desires, and take action to modify them if necessary.
- Effective people are able to establish their focus by clearly defining what they want and saying no to commitments that don't relate to those goals.
- Effective people anticipate problems. When they encounter an obstacle, they stay focused on their original goal and invest their energy in getting through the problem.
- Effective people surround themselves with supportive people. They clearly ask for the kind of help and encouragement they need, and they are willing to end relationships with destructive or unsupportive people.
- Effective people make their habits work for them. They are willing to identify patterns of behavior that could stop them from reaching their goals. When they identify a disempowering habit, they commit to replacing it with a more productive pattern.

KEEP STEPPING

LIVING IN BALANCE

Congratulations are in order! You have reached the conclusion of our process. While I hope each step in this program has helped you define and establish your own version of balance, I am even more hopeful that it has allowed you to get reacquainted with someone special—you.

Now that you've rediscovered the essence of the beautiful, powerful, passionate woman you are, I have another challenge for you. Make a decision—*right now*—that you will never lose yourself again. Commit to making time to stay connected with the authentic wisdom within you.

Never again allow your dreams to be put on hold by the expectations of others. Don't allow the quiet desperation of a silenced spirit to exist in your life. Instead, decide that you will use the skills you've learned in this program to create a life filled with joy, possibility, and meaningful contribution.

You were born with special gifts. Use them! You were born to embrace the experience of life—to learn, to teach, to grow, and to give. The world needs your talent, and the people in your life need your light.

Whether you realize it or not, you touch countless lives each day. The way you speak to your child teaches her about her own worth. The manner in which you interact with your co-worker can encourage her to apply her unique gifts, or it can teach her to hide them. The small acknowledgement you give to the clerk at your local market could be the difference between her feeling appreciated or invisible.

You are a pebble, thrown into the waters of life. Every action you take creates a ripple of response that touches the lives of those you come into contact with—and those whom they come into contact with. Create positive ripples!

This program has prepared you to live intentionally—mindfully interacting with others, using your talents to serve those around you, and living authentically. Listen to your life. It will talk to you. Follow your hunches. Take risks. Believe in something beyond you, and understand that your willingness to live a fulfilled and balanced life gives every person around you permission to do the same. That, in and of itself, is a service.

While this part of your exploration is ending, your real journey has only just begun! Your path of personal evolution and growth is a never-ending one. It winds through valleys of joyous discovery, and calls you to climb hills that will build your character. Walk with strength. Walk with faith. Walk with your head held high. And live every day as if it were your last. Honor yourself, and pursue your most deeply held wishes. The life of your dreams is before you.

GO GET IT!

TELL ME HOW YOU'RE DOING!

Would you like to be featured in one of my future books or on our website? Would you like to share your experience in working through this program with women around the world?

Please tell me your story!

I want to hear about how your life has changed. I want to hear about what you've learned, discovered, and overcome! When you write to me, I will personally read and respond to your communication, and I just may contact you to congratulate you personally!

Tell me all about your success! You can reach me by email at *kim_fulcher@mylifecompass.com*.

ABOUT THE AUTHOR

While some people operate on the basis of theory and information, Kimberly Fulcher writes, coaches, leads seminars, and speaks standing on the solid foundation of her experience in business and in life.

Kim's professional experiences range from the entrepreneurial—having co-founded a software company that ultimately sold for $38 million—to the executive—having successfully managed a national consulting company. She is the founder of Compass, Inc.—a coaching, training, and publishing company—and has served in executive advisory roles for several national coaching organizations.

Along the way, Kim has been profiled in numerous magazine articles and media features, and her own work is widely published. She is the co-creator of the popular audio program *Lead with Purpose. Live with Passion: A Femalepreneur's Guide to Small Business Success* and has most recently authored her first book, *Remodel Your Reality: Seven Steps to Rebalance Your Life and Reclaim Your Passion.* Kim's work is published throughout the Internet, and she has authored numerous e-books in support of her on-line coaching community, *www.mylifecompass.com.*

The power in Kim's approach comes from her ability to bring both men and women—from CEOs to small business owners to homemakers alike—back to the awareness of the underlying experience they're searching for. Once this essence is identified, she deftly guides them in creating practical, simple steps to achieve what they want in all areas of their life and work. As a result of her work, Kim has attained national recognition as an expert in personal and professional success.

Kim's own life is ample demonstration that she lives what she teaches. By walking her talk she has created a wonderful relationship with a loving husband, a happy blended family that includes four children between the ages of eight and nineteen, and a life of balance spent writing, coaching, running her business, speaking, and traveling between her home in California and her horse ranch in Washington State.

Kim is an avid fitness advocate, which translates across the human experience—impacting the physical, mental, emotional, and financial areas of life. Talk with Kim for more than a moment and you will understand that she is a woman who truly knows what she wants and enthusiastically pursues her passions.

STEP INTO FOCUS!
ENLIST THE SUPPORT OF A COACH
TO GUIDE YOUR GROWTH

You have invested a great deal of time, energy, and emotion in your *Remodel Your Reality* journey. You have just completed the initial process, and an unlimited future stretches out before you. I strongly encourage you to engage the support of our coaching community to help you stay on track! We have a number of options to provide you with the structure and motivation you'll need to stay your course.

Join Our Free Community

Each month our free community provides you with practical advice from leaders in the world of professional coaching and personal development, the support of women just like you, and the accountability that comes from making your goals public.

Become part of our free community! This is a no-cost way to connect with like-minded women, establish a built-in support structure, and receive gentle reminders to stay on your path.

Join a Compass Coaching Group

I am on a mission. I want every woman in the world to have a coach! I founded *www.mylifecompass.com* to make professional coaching accessible and affordable for women just like you. At Compass you can experience the power of working with a professional coach while bonding with a group of like-minded women. In fact, we make it possible for you to work with coaching programs designed to help you solve key problems in your life for just $19 per month. You can work with a professionally trained Compass Coach for as little as $39 per month. Give yourself the gift of inspiration, empowerment, and connection. Let us be your life compass! Find out more at *www.mylifecompass.com*.

Start a Compass Business

Women learn from other women. In fact, the most powerful role models in most women's lives are other women. If you are a man or woman who believes in the empowerment of women, I have a professional opportunity for you. Improve your life, and get paid for helping other women improve theirs! Find out more at *www.mylifecompass.com*.

Take Your Next Step Today!

Visit our on-line community and explore the many options we've created to support you in your ongoing journey of personal discovery and evolution!

www.mylifecompass.com

Compass, Inc.

5655 Silver Creek Valley Road, Suite 403

San Jose, CA 95138

Telephone: 866-341-8618

kim_fulcher@mylifecompass.com

www.mylifecompass.com

Learn a Bit More About Compass, Inc.

Compass, Inc., is a personal development company for women. We are the source for real and actionable information impacting every area of a woman's life. We envision a world where every woman has a coach. We commit to introduce coaching to women worldwide and to establish the world's leading coaching-based social network for women and personal development professionals.

Our on-line community for women provides self-help products and coaching programs to help our clients build happy lives and create fulfilling work. Our coaching services division works with small businesses and large corporations to guide individual employee development, create improvements in culture, and increase productivity.

www.mylifecompass.com

INDEX

A

abundance, 81–82
abuse, 28–31
acceptance
    habit of, 49–50
    need for, 64–66
    unconditional, 159
Action, Call to
    Analyze Your Change Personality, 168
    Apply the Seven Principles to Your Life, 160
    Assess Your Emotional Energy, 25–26
    Assess Your Mental Energy, 19–20
    Assess Your Physical Energy, 7–9
    Commit to Deepening Your Personal Intimacy, 154
    Create Your Attraction Profile, 94–95
    Define Your Priorities, 37–39
    Embrace Your Responsibility, 165
    Envision Your Ideal, 117–118
    Identify Your Core Values, 95–97
    Identify Your Passion Signals, 90
    Increase Your Emotional Energy, 31–32
    Increase Your Mental Energy, 24–25
    Increase Your Physical Energy, 18–19
    Map the Gap, 122
    Move Beyond the Common

    Blocks of Manifestation, 112
    Name Your Strengths, 87–88
    Satisfy Your Needs, 74
    Shift Your Beliefs, 82–83
    Shift Your Habits, 53–54
    Stay Focused, 170
    Take a People Inventory, 174
    Target Time Wasters, 47
    Your Essential Six Relationships, 141–142
actions, 26–27, 51, 69, 118–126
activities, 40–42. see also Call to Action
advocacy for self, 28–31, 72–73
Alise, client profile of, 139–140
Analyze Your Change Personality, 168
appearance, physical, 9
Apply the Seven Principles to Your Life, 160
Assess Your Emotional Energy, 25–26
Assess Your Mental Energy, 19–20
Assess Your Physical Energy, 7–9
assessment, self-, 120. see also Call to Action
assumptions, 159
attraction, 91–95
authority figures, 134–135
autonomy, 66–67
availability, 157

B

balance, 179–180, xxviii
bedtime. see sleep

behaviors. *see* habits
beliefs, 75–83
body, 7–9, 12–13, 13–14
boundaries, 42–43, 45–46, 72–73, 169
burnout, 16–18

C

calendar, 39–45
Call to Action. *see also* activities; self-assessment
  Analyze Your Change Personality, 168
  Apply the Seven Principles to Your Life, 160
  Assess Your Emotional Energy, 25–26
  Assess Your Mental Energy, 19–20
  Assess Your Physical Energy, 7–9
  Commit to Deepening Your Personal Intimacy, 154
  Create Your Attraction Profile, 94–95
  Define Your Passion Triad, 103
  Define Your Priorities, 37–39
  Embrace Your Responsibility, 165
  Envision Your Ideal, 117–118
  Identify Your Core Values, 95–97
  Identify Your Passion Signals, 90
  Increase Your Emotional Energy, 31–32
  Increase Your Mental Energy, 24–25
  Increase Your Physical Energy, 18–19
  Map the Gap, 122
  Move Beyond the Common

  Blocks of Manifestation, 112
  Name Your Strengths, 87–88
  Satisfy Your Needs, 74
  Shift Your Beliefs, 82–83
  Shift Your Habits, 53–54
  Stay Focused, 170
  Take a People Inventory, 174
  Target Time Wasters, 47
  Your Essential Six Relationships, 141–142
carbohydrates, 14
care, self-
  fundamentals of, 142–149
  habit of, 51
  lack of attention to, 4
  scheduling time for, 43–44
  self-worth and, 71–72
  vision and, 113–114
career, 116–117
categorization of tasks, 21–22
change, 165–168
chaos, 3–4
children, 11, 135–136
choice, 66
clarity, 108–112
cleaning, 7–12
client profiles
  Alise, 139–140
  Dana, 77–78
  Denise, 152–154
  Elaine, 156–157
  Erin, 166–168
  Hailey, 123–126
  Isabelle, 40–42
  Jennifer, 59–61
  Karen, 82–83
  Kathy, 57
  Keera, 77–78

Kelly, 171–174
Laura, 97–99
Mary, 16–18
Sharon, 132–134
clutter, 10–11
coaches, xxx
comfort, personal, 92–93
Commit to Deepening Your Personal
    Intimacy, 154
commitments
    assessing, 7–9
    autonomy and, 67
    boundaries and, 23–24
    to self, 73
    time management and, 40–42, 47
communication, interpersonal, 28–31
community, 65
compartmentalization, 113
Compass, Inc., xxx
competence, 68–70
connection, 64–66. *see also*
    relationships
constructiveness, unconditional,
    149–150, 150–151*f*
control, 63
courage, 109–111
Create Your Attraction Profile, 94–95
credit, to self, 152

D

Dana, client profile of, 77–78
Define Your Priorities, 37–39
Denise, client profile of, 152–154
departments, life, 113–117
desires, 120
diet, 9, 13–14
dreams

achieving, 126–127
action and, 118–126
clarity and, 108–112
designing of, 107–108
vision and, 112–118

E

eating habits, 9, 13–14
education, 69, 86, 93–94
effectiveness, personal
    change and, 165–168
    focus and, 169–170
    habits and, 174–176
    overview of, 163–164, 176–177
    personal responsibility and,
        164–165
Elaine, client profile of, 156–157
Embrace Your Responsibility, 165
emotional cues, 90
emotional energy. *see* energy
energy
    accounting for, 5–6
    emotional, 25–32
    importance of, 32–33
    mental, 20–25
    physical, 7–19
    plans and, 111–112
    types of, 6
entertainment, 91–92
environment, 7–12, 16, 18–19,
    115–116
Envision Your Ideal, 117–118
Erin, client profile of, 166–168
errands, 21–22, 24–25
excuses, 46
exercise, 15–16, 145–146
expectations for self, 23–24

experiences, 117

F

faith, 64, 109–111, 140–141, 145
family involvement in housekeeping, 11
family meetings, 17
family of origin, 164–165
fat, dietary, 14
fear, 109–111
feelings, 63
field trips, 147
finance, 63, 115
fitness. *see* exercise
focus, 169–170
forgiveness of self, 149
friends, 136–138, xxx

G

genuineness, 158
giving, 159–160
God. *see* faith
Golden Rule, 159–160
gratitude, habit of, 49
groups, support, xxx
growth, personal, 117

H

habits, 48–54, 63, 174–176
Hailey, client profile of, 123–126
health, 63
help, hired, 11–12
helplessness, 108–109
higher power. *see* faith
hired help, 11–12
hobbies, 91–92, 147–149

home environment. *see* environment
honesty, 28–29, 43
housekeeping, 7–12
husbands, 131–134
hydration, 12–13

I

Identify Your Core Values, 95–97
Identify Your Passion Signals, 90
inaction, ownership of, 27–28
inclusion, 65
Increase Your Emotional Energy, 31–32
Increase Your Mental Energy, 24–25
Increase Your Physical Energy, 18–19
independence, 67
intention, 99–104
interest in others, 158
interpersonal communication, 28–31
Isabelle, client profile of, 40–42

J

Jennifer, client profile of, 59–61
journaling, 144–145
joy, 94

K

Karen, client profile of, 82–83
Kathy, client profile of, 57
Keera, client profile of, 77–78
Kelly, client profile of, 171–174
kindness to self, 149–150
knowledge, 69, 86, 93–94

L

Laura, client profile of, 97–99
leisure, 91–92, 146–149
life, beliefs about, 77–78
limits. *see* boundaries
lists, 21–22, 24–25, 37–39
love, 65, 80–81. *see also* relationships

M

manifestation, 112
Map the Gap, 119, 122
Mary, client profile of, 16–18
material environment. *see* environment
mates, 131–134
meditation, 145
mental energy, 20–25
morality, 89
Move Beyond the Common Blocks of Manifestation, 112
music, 146–147

N

Name Your Strengths, 87–88
needs
    autonomy, 66–67
    competence, 68–70
    connection, 64–66
    neutrality of, 73–74
    overview of, 58–61, 83
    security, 61–64
    self-worth, 70–73
no, saying. *see* boundaries

O

obligations, 7–9, 23–24
obstacles, anticipating, xxix
opportunities, evaluation of, 45–46
organization, 10–11
outings, 147
outsourcing of household tasks, 11–12

P

parenting, 135–136
parents, 134–135
passion
    Define Your Passion Triad, 103
    empowering nature of, 85–86
    Identify Your Passion Signals, 90
    Laura, profile of, 97–99
    overview of, 104
    purpose, 99–104
    recipe for, 102
    strengths, 86–89, 103
    values, 89, 90, 103
people, beliefs about, 79–80. *see also* relationships
personal growth, 117
personal responsibility
    embracing, 164–165
    ownership of inaction, 27–28
    ownership of material environment, 11
    ownership of personal actions, 26–27
physical energy. *see* energy
physiological body, 7–9, 12–13, 13–14
plans, 111–112

play, habit of, 52–53
possibility, habit of, 49–50
potential, personal, 72
priorities, 36–39, 54
profiles. *see* client profiles
progress, 69–70
projects, 22–23, 25
protection, 63
protein, 13
purpose, 99–104

R

reading, 91
receiving, 159–160
recognition, 70
regrets, 27
rejection, 64, 140
relationships. *see also* connection; love
    acceptance, unconditional, 159
    assumptions and, 159
    availability and, 157
    with children, 135–136
    with empowering people, 171–174
    with friends, 136–138
    genuineness and, 158
    giving/receiving and, 159–160
    with a higher power, 140–141
    interest in others and, 158
    as life department, 114–115
    with mates, 131–134
    with parents, 134–135
    risk and, 155–157
    with self, 130–131, 142–149,
        149–154
    seven principles of, 155–160
    Your Essential Six Relationships,
        141–142
religion. *see* faith

resources, 121
responsibility, personal
    embracing, 164–165
    ownership of inaction, 27–28
    ownership of material environ-
        ment, 11
    ownership of personal actions,
        26–27
results, 121
risk, 155–157
routines, 39–45, 63

S

Satisfy Your Needs, 74
schedules, 39–45
security, 61–64
self, advocacy for, 28–31, 72–73
self-assessment, 120
self, beliefs about, 78–79
self-care
    fundamentals of, 142–149
    habit of, 51
    lack of attention to, 4
    scheduling time for, 43–44
    self-worth and, 71–72
    vision and, 113–114
self-connection, habit of, 52
self-depreciation, 70. *see also* self-
    worth
self-talk, negative, 152–154
self-worth, 44–45, 70, 143–144,
        149–154. *see also* needs
service, 100–101
seven principles of relationships,
        155–160
Sharon, client profile of, 132–134
Shift Your Beliefs, 82–83
Shift Your Habits, 53–54

shortcomings, acknowledging, 86
skills, 69, 86, 93–94
skincare, 9
sleep, 9, 14–15
space, personal. *see* environment
spirituality. *see* faith
spouses, 131–134
Stay Focused, 170
strengths, 86–89, 103
stretching, 16
structure, 21–22
success, 179–180
support system, xxx

T

Take a People Inventory, 174
takers, 45
Target Time Wasters, 47
task structuring, 21–22, 24–25
teaching, 93–94
thoughts, 75–83
time, 36, 39–45, 47
to-do lists, 21–22, 24–25, 37–39
triad, passion. *see* passion
truth, telling of the, 28–29

U

uncertainty, 109

V

values, 89, 90, 103
victimization, 28–31
vision, 112–118
vitality. *see* energy
volunteer activities, 40–42

W

walking, 15, 146. *see also* exercise
water, 9, 12–13
wealth, 81–82
weight, 9
weight loss, 171–174
wives, 131–134
work environment. *see* environment
worth, self-, 44–45, 59–61, 70–73
www.mylifecompass.com, xxx
www.internationalcoachfederation.
    org, xxx

Y

Your Essential Six Relationships,
    141–142

WWW.KIMBERLYFULCHER.COM